Shooter's Bible GUIDE TO EXTREME IRON

Shooter's Bible GUIDE TO EXTREME IRON

AN ILLUSTRATED REFERENCE TO SOME OF THE WORLD'S MOST POWERFUL WEAPONS, FROM HAND CANNONS TO FIELD ARTILLERY

STAN SKINNER

SKYHORSE PUBLISHING

Skyhorse Publishing books may be purchased in bulk at special discounts for sales promotion, corporate gifts, fund-raising, or educational purposes. Special editions can also be created to specifications. For details, contact the Special Sales Department, Skyhorse Publishing, 307 West 36th Street, 11th Floor, New York, NY 10018 or info@skyhorsepublishing.com.

Skyhorse® and Skyhorse Publishing® are registered trademarks of Skyhorse Publishing, Inc.®, a Delaware corporation.

www.skyhorsepublishing.com

10 9 8 7 6 5 4 3 2 1

Library of Congress Cataloging-in-Publication Data is available on file.

Cover design by Owen Corrigan
Cover photographs provided by Stan Skinner

ISBN: 978-1-62636-014-3
E-book ISBN: 978-1-62873-538-3

Printed in China

DISCLAIMER

Check your state and local laws before carrying a handgun, concealed or otherwise. Laws vary widely from state to state. Some states allow concealed carry without a permit, some require a permit, and some states do not allow concealed handgun carry at all. All states put restrictions on where and how handguns can be carried legally. In addition, several states outlaw particular modes of concealed carry. Your local law enforcement department or district attorney's office should know the details.

This book is not designed to take the place of a qualified and competent instructor; rather, it is a resource designed to supplement quality training.

CONTENTS

A Note from the Author

The premise of this book is that most of us will never own, have the opportunity to shoot, or even handle the guns you'll find in these pages. Some are outrageously expensive, some are so rare that it's unlikely that we'd ever physically see one or hold it in our hands. Others are so heavily regulated that few of us would subject ourselves to the tedious and onerous process of (legally) acquiring one. Most such guns would fall into more than one of these categories, which makes the problem even worse.

Let me make it clear that these obstacles apply to me as much as to anyone else. I do have a few nice toys of my own, but most of the guns in these pages are as far beyond my reach as yours.

This means I had to attend numerous trade shows and conventions to obtain interviews and photographs as well as to arrange consignment of firearms. I also visited various collectors and historians around the country to actually see, handle, and shoot some of the fascinating guns I've written about here.

Inevitably, I had to pick and choose among a seemingly endless list of guns that deserved mention. Mostly, I chose guns that interested me personally.

Almost without exception, there are many fascinating anecdotes and other tidbits to be told about these guns and/or categories of guns. I couldn't use them all, but I don't think you'll be disappointed with the choices I made.

Also, I would like to acknowledge those without whom I could not have written this book. Their encouragement, technical expertise, and able assistance were invaluable.

One in particular deserves special mention: Bill Ball has been a close friend since junior high school. Somehow, as we became adults, entered military service (Air Force for him, Army for me), married, and lived separate lives, we remained close friends and are still close to this day. We both are dyed-in-the-wool gun nuts who have hunted on several continents together and separately. We both are established authors, and I have benefited greatly from his expertise as I researched and wrote this book.

Many other friends and colleagues made valuable contributions to my research in ways too numerous to mention here. Nevertheless, each played a significant role in completing this project.

Alphabetically, these contributors are:

Bob Baker, president of Freedom Arms; Angela Barrett, director of marketing of Barrett Firearms; John Buhay, vice president, US Armament Corp; Laura Burgess, president Laura Burgess Marketing; Eric Burgess, vice president, Laura Burgess Marketing; George Caswell, owner Champlin Arms; Neil Davies, marketing director, Hornady; Everett Deger, marketing communications manager, Hornady; Alex Diehl, COO, Krieghoff Intl; Keith Duntze, McMillan Group Intl; Laura Evans, marketing coordinator, Crosman Corp.; Eric Graetz, founder, Lakeside Machine, LLC; Scott Grange, director of public relations, Browning Arms; Gary Giudice, owner Blue Heron Communications; Tyler Hartung, dyed-in-the-wool gun nut; Ed Hope, MG Shooters, LLC (Big Sandy); Garry James, author and firearms historian; J. D. Jones, author, cartridge designer and owner of SSK Industries; Ken Jorgensen, director of marketing, Sturm, Ruger; Dieter Krieghoff, president, Krieghoff Intl; Lon Laufman, owner RKL, Inc; Dave Mattausch (and entire family), master guides for Coues deer and desert bighorn sheep; Kelly McMillan, former owner, McMillan Group International; Jason Morton, marketing director, CZ-USA; Scott O'Brien, Steyr Arms/MerkelUSA; Randell Pence, senior sales executive, Sturm Ruger; Peter Pi, Sr., president, CorBon/Glaser; Paul Pluff, director of marketing services, Smith & Wesson; Dean Rumbaugh, company historian, Weatherby, Inc.; Mike Schwiebert, director of marketing, Weatherby Inc.; Mike Shovel, national sales manager, CorBon/Glaser; Blackie Sleewa, gun nut extraordinaire; Mike Strong, Pima Technologies; Kenton Tucker, MG Shooters, LLC (Big Sandy); Dwight Van Brunt, author; Mike Venturino, author and collector; Yvonne Venturino, firearms photographer.

Researching and writing *Shooter's Bible Guide to Extreme Iron* has been rewarding, but tedious, time-consuming, and seemingly never-ending. Still I am glad I had the opportunity to write this book, and I hope you'll enjoy reading it.

—Stan Skinner

I. Express Rifles

The rise of the classic express rifle is inextricably linked to the glory days of the British Empire when Queen Victoria's dominant military machine expanded the British Raj until one could truly say, "The sun never sets on the British Empire." As British adventurers penetrated to the darkest corners of Queen Vickie's Empire, they found a need for a powerful firearm capable of dispatching various large and dangerous beasts that inhabited these wild and remote places.

Black Powder Behemoths

Before the middle of the nineteenth century, the answer was found in muzzleloading black powder behemoths designed to fire lead balls that weighed as much as a quarter of a pound. A rifle firing a projectile of this size was known as a *four bore*. This naming system was identical to modern shotgun gauges. Just as a 12-gauge shotgun has a bore diameter able to hold a spherical lead ball weighing one-twelfth of a pound, a four bore gun could fire a spherical lead ball that weighed a full quarter-pound. Conical bullets were also used with great effect in these and smaller bore rifles.

Very few two-bore rifles were made, and they that were invariably single-shots. The smaller 8-bore generated considerably less recoil than the 4-bore, yet still generated adequate power for dangerous game. Smaller 10- and 12-bore rifles were mainly for medium to small game, but were marginal against the largest game.

Many early ivory hunters loaded these muzzleloaders with a handful of black powder carried loose in a convenient pocket. Then they rammed a lead ball or conical bullet over the powder charge. When this beast was touched off, a huge cloud of smoke issued from the muzzle as recoil rocked the shooter back on his heels.

A hunter stalking a herd of elephants could be in a tight spot after discharging his slow-to-reload muzzleloader. He had few options if he didn't kill his target animal quickly and it decided to charge.

Self-contained Cartridges

Around the middle of the century, self-contained, big-bore metallic cartridges loaded with heavy projectiles became available. These cartridges, still known by gauge diameter, were designed for breech-loading, side-by-side double rifles. The increased firepower of these new firearms quickly changed the face of hunting for Africa's dangerous game. Suddenly, ivory hunting was a considerably less-daunting prospect.

By the 1870s, higher-velocity centerfire cartridges such as the .500 Express (BPE) had emerged. Riflemaker James Purdey (the younger) coined the term *Express* to describe these cartridges, likening them to the speed and power of an express train. The .500 was a straight-cased, paper-patched cartridge offered in a half dozen lengths, ranging from 1.5–3 inches, and, later, 3.25 inches. The 3-inch version was the most successful. It was highly regarded in India and Africa for lions and tigers, but it was considered to be a "medium" cartridge—too light for rhinos and elephants.

A more satisfactory express cartridge for heavy, non-dangerous game was the .577 Express, which was introduced circa 1870. Its predecessors were variations on the British military cartridge, the .577 Snider. Offered in several lengths, the most successful was the 3-inch version.

Nitro Express Cartridges

In the last decade of the century, Cordite (a "double base" smokeless propellant of mostly nitrocellulose and nitroglycerin) had ushered in a dramatic improvement in express rifle cartridges. So, the "nitro express" family of cartridges quickly made their black powder antecedents obsolete.

One of the earliest nitro express cartridges was the .500 Nitro Express. Adapted in the 1890s from the .500 Black Powder Express to use Cordite propellant, the .500 NE uses a 570-grain bullet at 2,150 fps. It is considered to be among the most potent Africa cartridges even today.

▲ Arizona hunting guide Dave Mattausch is rocked back by the recoil of 570-grain bullet launched at 2,100 feet per second from a Merkel double rifle in .500 Nitro Express. Muzzle energy is 5,583 foot pounds.

In 1900, John Rigby developed the .470 Nitro Express, one of the first designed specifically for Cordite smokeless propellant. Reputedly, this cartridge was designed as a replacement for Rigby's earlier .450 NE because of a British ban on .45 caliber ammunition in India and the Sudan.

The .470 NE is still among the most popular double-rifle chamberings. Launching a 500-grain bullet at 2,150 fps, it is considered to be a better stopper than the .458 Winchester Magnum and is currently loaded by several major ammo manufacturers.

Like the .500 NE, the .577 Nitro Express was adapted from an earlier black powder cartridge. Rifles for this cartridge weigh thirteen pounds or more to contain the prodigious recoil of a 750-grain bullet leaving the .577 NE's muzzle at 2,050 fps. Many professional

ivory hunters favored the .577 NE over the larger .600 NE because of its reputation for greater penetration.

The most powerful of the nitro express cartridges was the .600 Nitro Express, which propels a 900-grain bullet at 1,950 fps and yields 7,500 foot pounds of energy at the muzzle. It was introduced by W. J. Jeffery & Company in their double rifles, but several other rifle makers soon offered .600 Nitro Express double rifles, as well. This remained the most powerful commercial sporting rifle cartridge for more than fifty years. Then, in 1957, Roy Weatherby developed his .460 Weatherby Magnum.

In 1988, Holland & Holland accepted a commission from a wealthy client to produce a double rifle in an even more powerful cartridge, the .700 Nitro Express. The story behind this commission is worth telling:

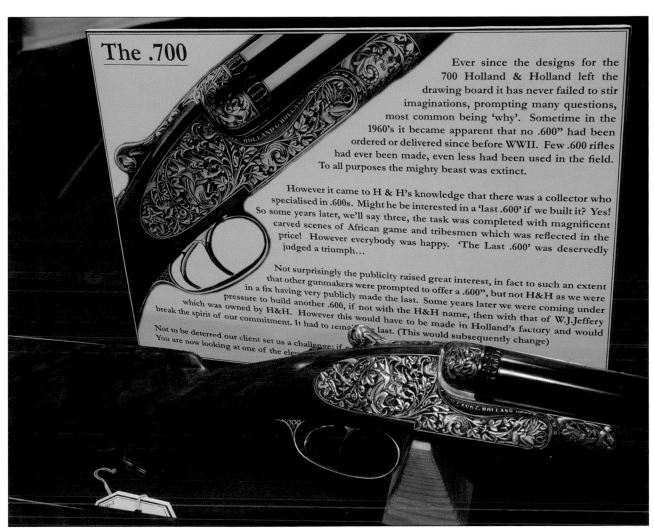

The .700

Ever since the designs for the 700 Holland & Holland left the drawing board it has never failed to stir imaginations, prompting many questions, most common being 'why'. Sometime in the 1960's it became apparent that no .600" had been ordered or delivered since before WWII. Few .600 rifles had ever been made, even less had been used in the field. To all purposes the mighty beast was extinct.

However it came to H & H's knowledge that there was a collector who specialised in .600s. Might he be interested in a 'last .600' if we built it? Yes! So some years later, we'll say three, the task was completed with magnificent carved scenes of African game and tribesmen which was reflected in the price! However everybody was happy. 'The Last .600' was deservedly judged a triumph...

Not surprisingly the publicity raised great interest, in fact to such an extent that other gunmakers were prompted to offer a .600", but not H&H as we were in a fix having very publicly made the last. Some years later we were coming under pressure to build another .600, if not with the H&H name, then with that of W.J.Jeffery which was owned by H&H. However this would have to be made in Holland's factory and would break the spirit of our commitment. It had to rema̶ ̶e last. (This would subsequently change)

Not to be deterred our client set us a challenge: if ...
You are now looking at one of the ele...

▲ This highly embellished Holland & Holland double rifle is chambered for the world's most powerful commercial sporting cartridge, the .700 Nitro Express

Some years earlier, Holland & Holland decided to end its production of .600 NE double rifles. The last rifle made was bought at a substantial premium with the company's agreement never again to make a rifle chambered for this cartridge. So in 1988, when Holland & Holland refused a client's request for a .600 NE double rifle, he countered by asking whether they would build a .700 Nitro Express. The company agreed.

Since then, the .700 Nitro Express has been offered by several rifle makers. The standard .700 NE load calls for a 1,000-grain bullet propelled at (or about)

▲ The yawning bores of a Holland and Holland .700 Nitro Express double rifle are impressive.

700 Nitro Express

The 700 NE was developed in 1988 by Jim Bell of Bells Basic Brass and William Feldstein of Beverly Hills, California. It is chambered in a limited number of double rifles made by Holland & Holland. It came about because Mr Feldstein wanted Holland & Holland to build him a 600 NE. They were unable to, because they had already completed their limited edition 600 NE's some years before, and were not interested in reviving this calibre. The 700 NE round carries a bullet weighing 1000 grains. With a muzzle velocity of 2000 fps it produces 8900 ft-lbs of muzzle energy.

▲ Unsurpassed among commercial sporting rifle cartridges, the Holland & Holland .700 Nitro Express is tipped with a 1,000-grain bullet. Muzzle velocity is 2,000 fps, which generates 8,900 foot pounds of energy at the muzzle.

2,000 fps which yields about 8,900 foot pounds of muzzle energy.

Nitro Express Double Rifles

With the advent of the nitro express family of cartridges, a standard pattern soon emerged for double rifles chambered for them. Elsewhere, a double gun might be an over/under or a combination rifle/shotgun, but for Africa's game, the break-open, side-by-side ruled.

This was because of the geometry of a break-open, over/under double rifle. The action must break open at a fairly steep angle to clear the bottom barrel for loading and ejection. A side-by-side could clear both barrels at a shallower angle, which, in theory, makes it a fraction faster and more reliable to reload in a tense situation.

▲ A side-by-side double rifle, such as this Krieghoff Classic Safari chambered for .470 Nitro Express, is considered faster to reload because it breaks open at a relatively shallow angle to eject fired cartridge cases and reload. In sharp contrast, an over/under double rifle must break open to a much steeper angle so the spent cartridge in the bottom barrel has clearance to eject. This makes an over/under inherently slower to reload than a side-by-side.
Photo credit: David Mattausch

▲ Unlike a relatively low-priced double rifle by Merkel, Krieghoff, or others, vintage rifles by upper crust British makers command eye-popping prices at firearms auctions and private sales. For example, this Holland & Holland Royal Ejector Model chambered for 500/465 Nitro Express can be yours for a mere $79,500.

For the same reason, a tang-mounted latching lever was preferred to a bottom or side lever. An iron sight with a large front head and "shallow vee" rear sight was *de rigueur* on most double guns chambered for nitro express cartridges. These sights were often silver-soldered in place to resist hard knocks in the field, although multiple folding leaves were sometimes installed for accurate shots at longer ranges.

Side-by-Side Action Types

Several proprietary double-rifle action designs by various gun makers have emerged, but most of them fall into two general types: sidelock and boxlock. Within these two types, there are several variations, which we will not go into here because of space limitations.

The sidelock action is generally reserved for better grade guns and has several technical advantages. These advantages have little discernible impact on performance in the field, so there is another reason why the sidelock action is preferred among carriage-trade. The sidelock action is a blank canvas for the work of a master engraver on often highly embellished double rifles. There are two variations of the sidelock action,

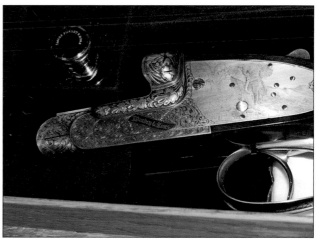

▲ This exhibition grade Purdey double rifle has full-coverage floral and scroll-work engraving along with African game scenes and a gold-inlaid maker's mark.

the "bar action" and the "back action." Each had its detractors.

The buttstock of the back action was inherently weaker because inletting the action required removing more wood right where it was needed to absorb the massive recoil of a cigar-sized elephant cartridge. On the other

▲ This left-hand Weatherby Mark V DGR is chambered for .460 Weatherby Magnum. It has a drop box magazine that increases capacity to three rounds in the magazine and one in the chamber. Unlike classic bolt-action express rifles, the magazine is not blended into the stock.

hand, the bar action necessitated machining cuts in the action bar, which supposedly weakened the action itself. Failures of either type were exceedingly rare, so these supposed drawbacks are mostly theoretical.

The sturdy, but plain, boxlock double rifle served less-affluent hunters, including virtually all commercial ivory hunters except those who preferred a bolt-action "magazine" rifle.

Bolt-action Express Cartridges

John Rigby, the third-generation head of the company bearing his name, negotiated a deal with Germany's Mauser Werke to be the sole agency for the bolt action 1898 Mauser in England and its colonies. He then designed the .416 Rigby cartridge for this action, and Rigby rifles chambered for this superb cartridge quickly established themselves as a first-rate choice for hunting Africa's dangerous game.

Another notable cartridge introduced in 1909 was the .404 Jeffery. This cartridge, which actually used a .423-inch bullet, is known in Europe as the 10.75x73mm. With a 400-grain bullet at a muzzle velocity just over 2,100 fps, the .404 Jeffery was less potent than

the original Cordite .416 Rigby load (410-grains at 2,300 fps), but generated significantly milder recoil. It was considered adequate for dangerous game and was issued to game department personnel in many of Britain's African colonies, with the exception of Uganda.

In 1911, the .505 Gibbs was introduced with a "rimless" cartridge case, which was well-suited for a bolt-action rifle. It was followed in 1912 by the .375 Holland & Holland Magnum, which employed a "belt" at the base of the case body. Although it was not the first belted cartridge, the .375 H&H Magnum chambered in a bolt-action "magazine" rifle swiftly proved to be an effective African "medium bore" cartridge. Aside from its ability to put down many of Africa's toughest big game species, the chief advantage of the bolt-action/.375 H&H Magnum combination was its three-round magazine capacity, which, with a chambered cartridge "up the spout," gave the hunter four fairly quick shots before it was necessary to reload.

The mighty .505 Gibbs, also introduced in 1911, enjoyed the same three-round magazine capacity of other bolt-action cartridges. However, this chambering

▲ Weatherby Mark V DGR (Dangerous Game Rifle) rifles use a shallow vee rear sight with a unique screw-thread elevation adjustment.

was an honest-to-God elephant caliber, rivaling the most powerful nitro express cartridges.

Several decades and two world wars later, American wildcatter and gunmaker Roy Weatherby gained prominence with his Weatherby magnum cartridges. His first entry into the express rifle cartridges was the .375 Weatherby Magnum, fireformed from the existing .375 H&H Magnum. The case wall was blown out to a minimum taper and the shoulder was formed into the distinctive Weatherby "double venturi" curves. The .375 Weatherby launches a 300-grain bullet at 2,800 fps. This is about 140 fps faster than the .375 H&H Magnum with a similar weight bullet.

In 1953, Weatherby upped the ante with a brand new express rifle cartridge, the .378 Weatherby Magnum. The cartridge case is belted like other Weatherby cases, but otherwise is similar in dimensions to the .416 Rigby. The new Weatherby boosts the muzzle velocity of a 300-grain bullet to 2,925 fps and generates a sharp recoil that has become legendary.

Winchester entered the express rifle fray in 1956 with its much-beloved Model 70 bolt-action chambered for a brand-new cartridge, the .458 Winchester Magnum. The new round was designed to equal .470 NE ballistics, generating 2,140 fps with a 500-grain bullet. It quickly became a favorite African chambering in European-made rifles as well as those by most American manufacturers. It is suitable for any of Africa's dangerous game, despite a problem with its ball propellant, which has long since been corrected.

Not to be outdone, Weatherby countered in 1958 with its .460 Weatherby Magnum, a necked-up .378 Weatherby. Chambered in the new Weatherby Mark V bolt-action rifle, it originally fired a 500-grain bullet at 2,700 fps. This generated more than 8,100 foot pounds of muzzle energy, surpassing the .600 Nitro Express. However in recent years, Weatherby has dialed back the .460 Weatherby to about 2,600 fps, which generates barely 7,500 foot pounds, but is still a formidable elephant stopper.

In the intervening years a staggering number of new express-rifle-class cartridges have emerged—far too many to list here. Many of them have carved out a niche while others have fallen into disuse and obscurity.

▲ Five of today's widely-used express rifle cartridges are (from left): the "medium power" .375 H&H Magnum, .416 Rigby and .470 Nitro Express, along with two heavy hitters, the .460 Weatherby Magnum and the .500 Nitro Express.

However, express rifles themselves, whether bolt-action or double rifle—even a few single shots—continue to capture the imagination of shooters, young and old.

Magazine (bolt-action) Express Rifles

Although other turn-bolt rifle actions emerged at various times in earlier decades, it was Paul Mauser who perfected perhaps the most significant advance in firearms of the nineteenth century. His Model 1871 was the first metallic cartridge firearm adopted by the German military. He continued to develop the concept through several evolutions until he unveiled his masterpiece, the Model 1898 Mauser bolt-action rifle.

By 1899, England's John Rigby & Co. made sporting rifles on the Model 98 action in .275 Rigby (the Anglicized 7x57mm Mauser) and .350 Rigby. Rigby later persuaded Mauser to redesign the 98 Mauser to accept longer cartridges. The result was the Magnum Mauser square bridge action, which became the basis for magazine express rifles by Rigby, Westley-Richards, and Jeffery. Rigby used this action for his .416 Rigby chambering, introduced in 1911.

Bolt-action express rifles became popular among many Africa hunters as a less expensive alternative to a double rifle chambered for one of the nitro express cartridges. Cartridges such as .375 H&H Magnum, .404 Jeffery, or .416 Rigby in a bolt action offered power equivalent to a nitro express chambering as well four shots before reloading instead of two.

The classic bolt action express rifle had several distinctive features that set it apart from other bolt-action sporting rifles. The most eye-catching feature was the "dropped" magazine. Because of the large case diameter of most express-rifle-class cartridges, the internal magazine extended down in front of the trigger guard to accommodate three cartridges. Accordingly, the forend and floor plate were designed to slope down to enclose the magazine, then arc up around the trigger guard and back along the wrist to meet the graceful curve of the pistol grip. This gave the rifle a brawny appearance that, no doubt, inspired many a hunter's confidence in the rifle.

Other distinctive features included a barrel band at the muzzle, which served as the base for the front sight. The sight itself consisted of a large (usually

warthog ivory) bead with a protective hood. The rear sight was a shallow vee that often boasted multiple folding leaves. This was either silver-soldered onto the barrel or sometimes inletted into a quarter rib.

Express rifles are available on bolt action platforms such as the Winchester Model 70, Weatherby Mark V, CZ 550 and numerous others. Each has features that set it apart from the others, but all are descendants of Paul Mauser's brainchild, the Model 1898 Mauser.

Express Rifles as Art

A finely crafted rifle or shotgun is, by itself, a thing of beauty, which often inspires its owner (if he can afford it) to have it embellished with elaborate engraving, precious metal or ivory inlays, even ornate wood carving. This art form dates back nearly to the invention of the gun, itself.

A best grade express rifle from a well-known maker of fine guns, fully embellished by a master craftsman, can command a price well into six figures. In a few exceptional cases, the price can climb to more than a million.

As the year 2000 approached, Safari Club International asked Holland & Holland to build one more .600 Nitro Express double rifle to be auctioned at the Year 2000 SCI Annual Hunters Convention. The company contacted the estate of the client who bought the last of the Holland & Holland .600 NE double rifles. The estate released H&H from their pledge, and the company agreed to build the .600 Nitro Express once again.

This rifle would be fully embellished by the best artisans available and would be the centerpiece of the gala banquet/auction on Saturday night at the end of the SCI Convention. Only the finest firearms and the most fabulous hunts would be auctioned at this final convention event—some of which would sell for more than $100,000.

About fifteen years earlier, a bolt-action masterpiece, the "Leopard Rifle" by Tucson riflemaker David Miller, brought a record $201,000 at the SCI Convention. This rifle was truly a showpiece crafted by Miller and his associate Curt Crum. Master engraver Lynton McKenzie, now deceased, contributed exquisite engraving with extensive gold inlays.

At the year 2000 SCI Convention, this record was to be surpassed by a large margin when the Holland & Holland .600 Nitro Express double rifle was gaveled at $270,000.

If your budget permits, you can obtain a fine, vintage double rifle by one of the legendary British gunmakers for about the same price as a spacious house in a nice neighborhood. Similar vintage bolt-action express rifles will cost about as much as a decent SUV, with a few costing as much as the price of a new Mercedes.

If you'd rather spend most of your disposable cash on an African safari for elephant or other dangerous game, several current manufacturers offer excellent, but more modestly priced, express rifles to accompany you on your hunt. You can choose from a fair number of potent chamberings suitable for everything from leopard to elephant. Many would be equally appropriate for a sojourn in Alaska for moose and grizzly bear. Let's take a look at some of these.

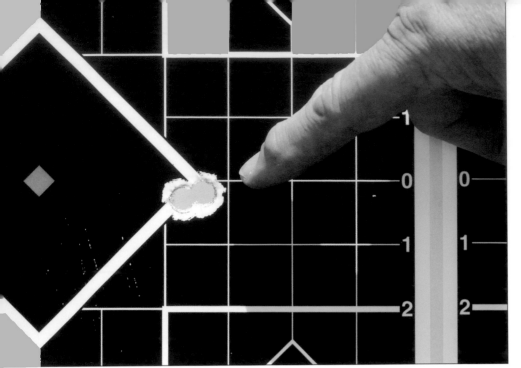

▲ The author fired a "quick left and right" with a Merkel 140 Safari double rifle chambered for .500 Nitro Express with the above result. One or two taps to drift the rear sight left just a tad will put rounds right where they'd spoil a Cape buffalo's whole day.

Current Double Guns

Besides the legendary British gunmakers, today's Africa hunters can choose from several makers of double rifles from Europe as well as the United States. Two of Europe's best double-rifle makers are Merkel and Krieghoff. We were fortunate to be able to take a Merkel and a Krieghoff double rifle to the range. The Merkel was a Model 140 Safari in .500 Nitro Express and the Krieghoff Classic in .470 Nitro Express.

The Merkel fits the definition of "classic" in every way; it has a boxlock action with extensive, well-executed arabesque engraving and game scenes on both sides. On the left side is a bull elephant while a Cape buffalo bull graces the right side.

▲ This Merkel .500 Nitro Express double rifle is a fine example of a "classic" side-by-side double rifle. Classic features include a multi-leaf, shallow vee rear sight, side pivoting locking lever, and tang-mounted safety.

▲ This modern express double rifle by Merkel of Suhl Germany offers all the traditional features an Africa hunter could want for a price under $10,000. It is chambered for a powerful "stopper" cartridge, the .500 Nitro Express.

Like most double rifles, the Merkel has a double trigger. This is considered to be more reliable because the two sides are completely separate, meaning that a malfunction of one side does not affect the other side, leaving it still able to fire. On the receiver, tang was a conventional sliding safety.

The Anson & Deeley–type action locks into battery with double underlugs while a Greener crossbolt provides a third point of contact. A half-inch wide, solid rib has a shallow vee rear sight with two folding leaves dovetailed into it and a small bead front sight.

The dark caramel-colored walnut stock was straight-grained with attractive black stripes throughout the butt and fore stock. Inletting was near-perfect, even where the buttstock joined the rear action wall, which was gracefully scalloped in the distinctive Merkel fashion.

Holding the Merkel firmly into my shoulder, I leaned into the gun and touched off a quick left and right. The recoil of the first shot rocked the barrels up and back under the massive recoil as I fought to bring the sights level for the second shot. As the rifle roared a second time, I again felt a massive push that nevertheless was quite tolerable. A quick trip downrange revealed two half-inch holes touching—right where they needed to be.

Properly shouldered, the Merkel chambered for the .500 Nitro Express will not hurt you, although expending a full box of .500 NE ammo will have you ready to call it a day. We soon received some help in this department.

At most public ranges, an unusual rifle will attract the attention of other shooters. Neither the Merkel nor the Krieghoff were exceptions to this rule, so we put the onlookers to work.

Some of the shooters had had enough after one shot, but others took the heavy recoil in stride and came back for more. Most were impressed with the classic

Merkel and the Krieghoff—also a classic. However, the Krieghoff incorporated a couple innovations that set it apart from other double rifles.

Krieghoff provided their Classic Safari double rifle chambered for .470 Nitro Express. It came in a handsome aluminum case, which also held a set of 20-gauge shotgun barrels and a Swarovski variable power riflescope.

Like the Merkel, the Krieghoff had a straight-grain, walnut stock with narrow, black stripes that contrasted sharply with a rich, dark background. The forend tapered to a graceful schnabel, giving it a more continental look. The boxlock action is less lavishly engraved than the Merkel, but lying atop the action

tang is one of the most important innovations since the transition from muzzleloaders to breechloaders: the cocking lever.

Resembling a somewhat oversize tang safety, the Krieghoff cocking lever renders a safety obsolete on any break-open-type firearm so-equipped. With the cocking lever, the shooter can nudge it forward with thumb pressure to take control of the cocked hammers. Then, easing the lever to the rear position de-cocks both barrels. When ready to fire, the shooter pushes the lever forward to re-cock both barrels.

This allows a hunter to carry the Krieghoff loaded, but uncocked unlike ordinary double rifles, which are

▲ A cocking lever on this Krieghoff .470 NE replaces the tang-mounted sliding safety found on most shotguns and modern double rifles. Once the rifle is loaded and the action closed, the cocking lever can be used to ease the hammers down to the uncocked position for safe carrying. When it is time to shoot, push the cocking lever forward to re-cock the hammers, and you are ready to fire.

▲ Krieghoff cut out the traditional shallow vee express rifle sight to Increase the area visible to the shooter without sacrificing quick target acquisition. It works perfectly.

fully cocked when loaded and rely on a sliding safety to prevent an accidental discharge.

The second noteworthy Krieghoff innovation is its shallow vee rear sight, with the inside cut away, unlike a conventional rear sight, which blocks a significant part of the target area as the shooter takes aim. Common sense tells me this feature would be faster to use in a tense situation.

As mentioned earlier, the Krieghoff came in an aluminum case with a Swarovski riflescope tucked alongside it. Because the purpose of an express rifle is to deliver a killing shot at close range, I don't regard a high-range variable power scope as either necessary or desirable. So, I did not try it on the Krieghoff. However, the 20-gauge shotgun barrels did pique my interest.

A trip to the local Trap and Skeet Club seemed in order. Upon arrival, I assembled the Krieghoff with the 20-gauge barrels and headed to an unoccupied trap station. A swipe of my card activated the trap house and the acoustic puller, so I stepped to the 16-yard line. Upon completing a round of trap, I was impressed. I had just broken 24 of 25 birds, which was about as well as I was capable of shooting.

More interesting was the fact that the Krieghoff side-by-side was definitely not a trap gun. More interesting still was the fact it was a 20-gauge, not a 12, not to mention that it didn't merely break birds—most of them were obliterated into powder. That's a nice bonus for what is first and foremost an elephant gun.

Current Bolt-action Express Rifles

After more than a century of refinement, today's dangerous game hunter has numerous options when choosing a bolt-action express rifle. After all that time, a fair number of currently manufactured bolt-actions are still virtually identical to the Mauser 98. Most of the others employ key features of that classic design.

▲ Some bolt-action express rifles follow the traditional pattern like the Dakota M76 Safari Model in .375 H&H Magnum at far right and the CZ 550 Magnum Express in .416 Rigby, second from right. Others, such as the Weatherby Mark V DGR in .460 Weatherby Magnum wears a polymer stock. The CZ 550 Magnum Express in .505 Gibbs and the big Weatherby Magnum both generate tremendous recoil, and both sport muzzle brakes to soften the blow. Note that three of the four are on left-hand actions, another recent innovation.

▲ This left-hand CZ 550 American Safari Magnum is chambered for .375 H&H Magnum. The action is a classic double square bridge Mauser with a single set trigger. A drop magazine holds four rounds with a fifth round In the chamber. A scope can be mounted on the CZ 550, using the 19mm dovetail on the receiver rings. Purists will prefer to use the multi-leaf, shallow vee rear and bead front sight.

Rifles such as the CZ 550 Safari Classic have a Mauser-type double square bridge action, controlled-round feed, dropped magazine and express sights just like those made a century ago, except for an optional modern muzzle brake. Oddly, it has a single set-trigger, which seems out of place on a rifle chambered for dangerous game cartridges, including the .505 Gibbs.

The Dakota 76 African differs from the classic express rifle pattern only by substituting an action similar to the Winchester Model 70. Otherwise, its graceful lines and nicely figured English walnut stock allow it to fit right in with British express rifles that cost many thousands more.

McMillan Firearms offers two bolt-action models that carry on the African express rifle tradition with distinctly modern features, including a stainless steel barrel and fiberglass stock. Both models use a McMillan custom action with a classic dropped magazine. The Heritage model is designed for use with a riflescope and does not have iron sights. The Prestige model employs the classic shallow vee rear sight with one folding leaf and a barrel-band mounted front sight with a fiber optic bead.

The Weatherby DGR (Dangerous Game Rifle) charts its own path in express rifles, beginning with the distinctly different Weatherby Mark V push-feed action. The DGR has a synthetic stock and a dropped magazine that, unlike other dropped magazines, is not faired into the front of the trigger guard. Even the shallow vee rear express sight displays Weatherby's innovative thinking. Instead of folding leaves for elevation adjustment, the Weatherby sight uses a tiny knurled wheel and angled screw thread to elevate the sight blade, which travels in a sturdy channel to resist the enormous recoil of Weatherby's proprietary cartridges. Unlike the other bolt-action express rifles discussed above, the Weatherby Mark V DGR is available only in Weatherby's proprietary chamberings including the .375, .378, .416, and .460 Weatherby magnums.

All of the contemporary bolt-action express rifles described above share one feature unknown in the express rifles of a hundred years ago: They are all available in a left-hand model, a fact that endears them to me and my fellow southpaws everywhere.

▲ The CZ 550 American Safari Magnum uses a robust multi-leaf shallow vee sight, which is pre-set for 100, 200, and 300 yards.

Which is best: Bolt or double?

One enduring controversy is debated even today: which is best for the heaviest African big game species, the bolt-action magazine rifle or the more traditional, side-by-side double rifle?

The double rifle is unsurpassed in delivering two quick shots. Although a bolt-action rifle is somewhat slower to operate, in the hands of an experienced hunter, it can put four shots into a belligerent beast (or beasts) in short order.

In the days of the ivory hunters, these differences had more meaning than they do now. Then, the object was to collect as much ivory as possible. The hunter would stealthily approach a herd of elephants, needing to put as many of the animals on the ground as possible. After a "quick left and right," the hunter might have two elephants down, but find himself in the midst of the panicked survivors with an unloaded gun.

If the hunter had a staunch gunbearer beside him holding a second gun, he could be back in action quickly, ready to take more ivory or defend against a charging beast bent on revenge. However, if the hunter was unlucky, the gunbearer might lose his nerve and bolt for safer ground, taking the second gun with him.

If this happened, the hunter's best chance of survival was a swift reload. With a cool head and good manual dexterity, a hunter could press the action lever, allowing the action to break open.

If the gun had automatic ejectors, stout springs would sling the empty cases over the hunter's shoulder. With two fresh cartridges tucked between the fingers of his support hand, the hunter could then swiftly slip them into the empty breech, slam the action shut, and be ready to deliver another "quick left and right."

Maybe.

So, I don't know the answer to "Which is best?" I know which type I prefer, but only you can say what's best for you.

II. Hand Cannons

❝ . . . but being this is a forty-four magnum, the most powerful handgun in the world and would blow your head clean off, you've got to ask yourself one question: 'Do I feel lucky?' Well, do ya, punk?"

This famous line from the 1971 movie *Dirty Harry* instantly elevated America's fascination with hand cannons to a whole new level. Of course, this fascination existed long before *Dirty Harry*. More than 160 years ago, Captain Samuel H. Walker collaborated with Samuel Colt to design a new revolver for use by the Texas Rangers and US Army dragoons.

The Colt Walker Revolver

Unlike the earlier Colt Paterson five-shot revolver, the Colt Walker revolver would have six chambers and a fixed trigger, setting a pattern that is prevalent in revolvers even today. It would also shoot a larger caliber than the Paterson, over a heavy powder charge designed to be equally deadly to an enemy cavalryman and to his horse.

The Colt Walker measured nearly 16 inches long, weighed 4.5 pounds, and would be carried in a saddle holster. A normal load consisted of a 146-grain round ball over 60 grains of black powder, which generated up to 1,200 fps and more than 500 foot pounds of energy at the muzzle. Primitive metallurgy, and (probably) careless loading practices, caused nearly three hundred Walker cylinders to rupture in service. These were returned to Colt for repair, and as a result, Colt recommended reducing the powder charge to 50 grains.

Only one thousand Walker Colts were manufactured for the military, along with about one hundred commercial models delivered to Samuel Colt. Colt used many of these for presentation to various prominent individuals. This included Samuel Walker, who received his pair of Walker Colts in 1847, scant days before his death in battle during the Mexican War.

The Colt Walker's success launched Colt's Patent Firearms Manufacturing Co. as a commercial success that continues even today. The Colt Walker enjoys one additional distinction: until the advent of the .357 magnum

▼ The Colt Walker revolver, introduced in 1847, reigned supreme as the world's most powerful handgun until 1934 when Smith & Wesson unveiled the .357 S&W Magnum in a modern double-action revolver. The Walker's 4.5 pound heft helps tame the recoil of a 141 grain, .454 caliber lead ball traveling at well over 1,000 fps. By comparison, the 1911A1, at 2.4 pounds, is little more than half the weight of a Colt Walker.
Photo credit: Yvonne Venturino

nearly ninety years later, the .44 caliber Colt Walker reigned as the most powerful handgun in the world.

Meanwhile in the British Empire

As Britain's colonial rule expanded during the reign of Queen Victoria, thousands of British soldiers and colonists followed the Union Jack into some of the most remote regions of the earth. In Africa, India, and elsewhere, British military officers and aristocracy found hunting dangerous game to be the preferred manly sport.

One popular hunting method in India involved assembling as many as a hundred "beaters"—sometimes more—in a long line cordoning off a section of forest. At a signal, the beaters would make a deafening racket by shouting, beating metal pans, blowing horns, etc.

Hearing the sudden clamor, any animals inside the cordon would instinctively retreat from the noise. As the confused animals moved away, they would encounter impassable terrain features, nets, and other obstacles funneling them toward an open glade that seemed to promise escape.

As the beaters moved forward, continuing to make a horrendous din, the confused animals would retreat. Some of them would be in open panic, others merely ambling along, trying to escape the noise behind them.

Unbeknownst to the fleeing animals, several hunters would be stationed at shooting positions beyond the glade. Ideally, the hunters would be elevated, where they could see down into high grass or underbrush. A high rock outcropping or a *machan* (shooting platform) in a tree often served this purpose.

If available, the preferred shooting position was atop an elephant trained to remain steady upon gunfire. A handler, or *mahout*, usually sat astride the elephant's neck while the sportsman rode on the elephant's back inside a box-like saddle, called a *howdah*.

The howdah was generally equipped with seats. The more luxurious ones had cushions, ornate rugs, and a canopy to protect a delicate British complexion from the harsh subtropical sun. Usually a wicker basket containing a selection of chutneys and curries was on hand, as were suitable libations to help while away the time.

As the beat progressed, the sportsman might draw a bead on a sambar deer or a chital (axis deer) as they dashed across the clearing. Often, a wild boar would trot out, muttering his annoyance with porcine grunts and squeals. Sometimes, a boar would break back through the line of beaters, leaving panicked and injured beaters in his wake. Occasionally, a furtive leopard would streak past, scarcely giving the shooters time to raise their guns before he was gone.

Rarely, a Himalayan sloth bear might make a surly appearance, but all of these game animals, desirable as they were, sometimes were allowed to escape unmolested. On these occasions, the hunters would be focused on a more formidable quarry—the Bengal tiger.

During the nineteenth century, the Bengal tiger numbered in the many thousands throughout India and the rest of the Asian subcontinent. The largest of the big cats, Bengal tigers possessed enormous strength. They were quite intelligent and equipped with formidable teeth and claws. In the blink of an eye, a tiger could spring from an ambush ten yards away and overpower its prey with slashing claws and a crushing bite. Also, Bengal tigers were athletic, easily capable of leaping high enough to reach an elephant's back.

As the clamor and din of the beaters approached, a tiger would feel a rising anger. Fearing nothing in the jungle, the tiger would deeply resent being rousted from its repose. Sometimes the tiger would turn and charge the line of beaters. Often, the big cat would maul one or more of the beaters severely before making its escape. More often, the big cat would give ground ahead of the beaters, confused and angry. As its rage multiplied, it might turn back growling, claws extended, then crouch and lunge toward its tormenters in frustration before striding stiffly away.

In time, it would reach the open glade and pause, reluctant to leave the concealing undergrowth. The tiger's sharp eyes would soon pick out the hunter waiting on elephant-back, and its cunning mind would realize instantly that this was the real enemy.

In a heartbeat, the tiger would leap into action, racing into the open away from the hunter in a desperate attempt to escape—*sometimes*. If the tiger were sufficiently enraged, it might instead focus on the puny creature atop the elephant. Often the hunter's first glimpse of the tiger was a black-striped orange blur streaking toward him, its jaws agape.

If the hunter were alert and skilled, a swift left and right with his express rifle would crumple the tiger in mid-charge. However, if he were slow to react, or if his shots had been wide of the mark, his day might turn out very badly.

The Howdah Pistol

That's where the howdah pistol came in. Derived from earlier muzzle-loading pistols, the howdah pistol was intended as a last-ditch defense if a leaping, enraged tiger were to join the hunter in his howdah.

Because a howdah could become very crowded with one or more hunters sharing space with a 600-pound tiger, the howdah pistol had to be compact and ready to fire instantly in what would certainly be a lively melee.

An enraged tiger was capable of reducing a man to his component parts in milliseconds. Therefore, a low-powered cartridge would not do. A howdah pistol had to chamber a large-bore, full-powered cartridge with stopping power capable of an instant lights-out result.

To be useful dispatching a tiger, a howdah pistol must remain loaded at all times. Yet it had to withstand the lurches and rolls of an elephant's gait and incidental knocks during a full day of hunting without discharging accidently.

These constraints defined a howdah pistol's form within fairly limited parameters. So, fairly short barrels were necessary—at least two of them as insurance

▼ This double-barrel howdah pistol, chambered for .577 Snider, is owned by firearms historian and author, Garry James. It was made by R. B. Rodda & Co. of London and Calcutta. It is a fine example of the nineteenth-century gunmakers' art. To open the action for loading, the shooter rotates the underlever a quarter turn counterclockwise.

▲ Garry James's howdah pistol is chambered for the .577 Snider British service cartridge. Fired from a British-issue Snider Enfield rifle, the .577 Snider launched a 480-grain lead bullet at about 1,300 fps. Fired through a short-barreled howdah pistol, performance was reduced considerably, but it would still be potent medicine for an angry tiger at close range.

against a misfire or errant shot. A few howdah pistols had four barrels, but most were of conventional side-by-side, double-barreled design.

The most common chamberings were two British military rifle cartridges, the .577 Snider and the .577/.450 Martini-Henry. These full-power cartridges offered great stopping power at contact range, but with a recoil level that could be controlled easily with a one-handed grip. In later years, some so-called howdah pistols were offered in lesser cartridges and were popular to some extent.

Outside hammers with prominent hammer spurs allowed a howdah pistol to be carried uncocked for safety, yet the hammers could be cocked quickly, bringing the gun into action without delay.

Although hammerless double guns had become available in the 1880s, outside hammers remained the most popular form for a howdah pistol, probably because a loaded hammerless gun is necessarily fully cocked and must rely on a safety that might be hard to locate and disengage with a Bengal tiger in your face.

Well-known firearms historian Garry James offered me an opportunity to fire his vintage howdah pistol and several other guns from his collection. Garry's pistol conforms to the general pattern described above. Made by English gunmaker Lancaster for Rodda of Calcutta, it is a short-barreled side-by-side chambered for .577 Snider. This compact piece has double triggers and outside hammers with large hammer spurs that can be cocked quickly. An underlever that wraps around the trigger guard swings sideways to open the action for loading and unloading.

▲ During a visit to Kalispell, Montana, I had a chance to try out a double-barreled howdah pistol chambered for .577 Snider. Recoil was a heavy push that caused a significant muzzle flip. I recovered quickly and touched off a second aimed shot a fraction of a second later. *Photo credit: Gary James*

It is a beautiful firearm, but as they say, "Beauty is as beauty does." So, it was time to put this beauty to the test. A leisurely afternoon at a shooting range near Garry's home in Montana soon confirmed that this fine example of a nineteenth-century British gunmaker's art does very nicely, indeed. It nestled nicely in my hand and was both pleasant and fun to shoot.

As a final note, despite the fact that I enjoyed shooting Garry's howdah pistol and the fact that it, or others like it, was probably carried on many tiger hunts, I could not find a single recorded instance where one was actually used to kill a tiger that attacked a hunter in a howdah on an elephant's back. My search notwithstanding, I believe it could have happened, probably many times. I certainly hope it did.

The .357 Magnum—A Modern Hand Cannon

More so than Europeans, Americans have appreciated relatively high-powered, large bore handguns dating back even before the introduction of the Colt Walker .44-caliber revolver in 1847. However, it wasn't until 1935 that the modern era of hand cannons began.

In that year, Smith & Wesson introduced the .357 Smith & Wesson Magnum, which surpassed the Walker both in muzzle velocity and in muzzle energy despite its smaller caliber. Touted as being able to penetrate and disable an automobile engine block, the .357 Maggie can trace its lineage to noted gun writer Elmer Keith who experimented with souped-up .38 Special handloads in a .44-caliber-frame S&W revolver (known much later as the "N" frame).

Keith had the large-frame revolver fitted with a custom barrel and cylinder chambered for .38 Special. He then developed high velocity loads at equally high pressures that would have been unsafe to fire in smaller-frame, factory standard .38 Special revolvers. This evolved into the .38-44 High Velocity cartridge, with an operating pressure roughly twice that of the .38 Special.

In 1935, Smith & Wesson introduced the .357 S&W Magnum, which was developed by S&W's Daniel B. Wesson II with the assistance of Phil Sharpe, a well-known firearms authority. The .357 was based on the .38 Special cartridge lengthened one-tenth of an inch so it would not chamber in a standard .38 Special revolver. The new cartridge had a muzzle velocity of 1,250 fps with a 158-grain bullet, which made it the most powerful handgun in the world until the introduction of the .44 S&W Magnum in 1955. This soon became Smith & Wesson's bestselling revolver despite its significantly higher price tag. Even Dick Tracy used the .357, drilling numerous engine blocks in the getaway cars of desperate, comic-strip crooks in the Sunday funnies.

The .44 S&W Magnum

Having been instrumental in the development of the .357 S&W Magnum, Elmer Keith once again turned the handgun world on its ear by playing a key role in development of the .44 Remington Magnum. His idea for the new cartridge emerged from his experiments with the .44 Smith & Wesson Special, which had been developed in 1907 as a replacement for the then-popular .44 Russian.

Although the earlier offering had a reputation for fine accuracy as a black-powder cartridge, its limited powder capacity was deemed unsuitable for the bulky smokeless powder available then. As a result, the .44 Special was designed with a significantly greater case capacity and stronger cartridge case.

Unfortunately, factory ammo merely duplicated that of the earlier cartridge, so it languished and never achieved much acceptance until it caught Keith's eye. Taking advantage of the larger and stronger case, Keith began stretching the .44 Special's pressure boundaries and achieved impressive results.

Armed with his .44 Special test data, Keith approached Smith & Wesson about offering a commercial version of his high-pressure loads along with revolvers chambered for it. Smith & Wesson eventually was persuaded and collaborated with Remington to develop a new cartridge based on the .44 Special.

As with the earlier .357 Magnum, the new cartridge, named .44 Remington Magnum, was designed to be slightly longer than the parent round to prevent it being loaded in revolvers chambered for .44 Special.

The first Smith & Wesson .44 Remington Magnum revolver was built in December 1955 and publicly announced in January 1956. Meanwhile Sturm, Ruger & Co. was not asleep at the switch. After a Ruger employee had found discarded, fired .44 Mag brass, the company did a bit of research and quickly adapted their Blackhawk revolver to the new round and put it into production. As a result, Ruger Blackhawk .44 Magnum revolvers actually reached dealer shelves a few weeks before Smith & Wesson's new .44.

Magnumania

The shooting public reacted favorably but warily to the powerful new handguns and their intimidating recoil. A small group of aficionados embraced the .44 Magnum eagerly, but most law enforcement agencies considered it briefly, then rejected it, deeming its weight and recoil too much for the average officer to carry and use effectively. Most other shooters reacted with little more than curiosity tempered by reluctance to experience what was becoming legendary recoil.

Then, a decade and a half later, something odd happened.

America was in turmoil. The Vietnam War had cost the lives of thousands and maimed even more. Violent protests had erupted on University campuses, and race riots had crippled cities on both coasts while rampant crime ravaged inner cities.

It seemed that America was coming apart at the seams. We needed a hero to strike back at the dark forces engulfing America and exact payback for their crimes and excesses. Then, like an avenging angel, a hero appeared.

His name was Harry Callahan.

▲ The Ruger Blackhawk revolver (top, in photo) in .44 Remington Magnum has a six-shot capacity while Freedom Arms Model 83 chambered for .454 Casull has only five. As a result the M83 has significantly thicker chamber walls than the Ruger Blackhawk. This enables it to safely handle .454 Casull chamber pressures nearly twice that of the .44 Remington Magnum.

But this hero did not wield a flaming sword. Instead, in his upraised fist, Dirty Harry held ". . . the most powerful handgun in the world"—a Smith & Wesson .44 Magnum revolver.

As Harry and his mighty .44 Magnum cut a bloody swath through hordes of evildoers in several movies, he made America's day. Meanwhile, thousands of shooters embraced Harry's choice of weapon, and sales of Smith & Wesson .44 Magnum revolvers skyrocketed. In a matter of weeks, the price of these revolvers tripled as the manufacturer strove to meet a surging demand.

In the real world, little had actually changed, except one thing. Like hotrods and supersonic jets, we had fallen in love with magnum handguns. We wanted them with a passion—and the bigger the better.

The .454 Casull

It turns out that *Dirty Harry* was wrong. Since 1957, the most powerful handgun in the world was the .454 Casull, not the .44 Remington Magnum. Developed by Dick Casull and Jack Fulmer, the .454 Casull followed the pattern established by the .357 and .44 magnums by strengthening an existing case to handle high pressure and lengthening it so the cartridge could not fit a revolver chambered for the parent cartridge.

In this instance, the parent cartridge was the .45 Colt, and the .454 Casull case was 1.383 inches long, about one-tenth of an inch longer than the .45 Colt. With an operating peak pressure of 50,000 psi, this cartridge could drive a 250-grain bullet to a muzzle velocity of nearly 1,700 fps, generating about 1,600 foot-pounds of energy.

Casull needed a new, stronger revolver to contain the enormous chamber pressure the .454 would generate. So, he designed a single action with a slightly larger diameter, five-shot cylinder, which allowed thicker chamber walls than a smaller, six-shot cylinder would. This also allowed the bolt lock recesses at the rear of the cylinder to be offset between chambers instead of directly over the thinnest part of the chamber walls, further improving the cylinder's strength.

Casull's design became the Freedom Arms Model 83 five-shot, single-action revolver. Handguns made by this small Wyoming company are precision, hand-fitted works of art with price tags almost three times that of a more ordinary revolver. As a result, the .454 Casull reached only those relatively few shooters who were willing to pay for Freedom Arms quality.

Despite the price, some handgun hunters have used the Model 83 in .454 Casull to hunt big game, particularly dangerous game. A few have used the .454's smack down power to bring down a Cape buffalo or even an elephant.

I doubt that I will ever experience the dubious thrill of staring down a Cape buffalo with naught but a .454 Casull revolver in my hand. However, I do find it comforting to feel the weight of my Model 83 nestled in a shoulder holster while I cast a fly into a salmon stream in Alaska's brown bear country.

Hand Cannons Get Bigger

Even before *Dirty Harry*, another challenger was preparing to wrest the Most Powerful Handgun title away from the S&W .44 Magnum. This challenge came from the fertile imagination of J. D. Jones, a well-known firearms experimenter and gun writer. J. D.'s ideas had already made an impact on high-performance handgun ammo as early as the 1960s when he teamed up with Lee Jurras to develop high velocity loads for auto-pistols and revolvers. This ammo, marketed under the brand name Super Vel, used a relatively lightweight bullet at very high muzzle velocity to achieve a reputation as law enforcement and self-defense ammo.

In 1969, J. D. turned his efforts to the recently introduced Thompson/Center Contender. This single-shot pistol with its break-open action was not a cutting-edge design, but there was nothing like it widely available to the American shooter. It grew steadily in

▲ The author shoots a custom Thompson/Center Encore "hand cannon" built by J. D. Jones, owner of SSK Industries, Winterville, OH. It is chambered for .50 Alaskan, a wildcat cartridge based on a necked-up and shortened .348 Winchester. The scope is a Bushnell Elite 2-6X handgun scope using J. D.'s T'SOB rings and base. *Photo credit: J. D. Jones*

popularity as a hunting handgun, and J. D. found it to be a perfect platform for developing wildcat cartridges for handgun hunting.

In 1977, J. D. founded SSK Industries to build and market products related to handguns and ammunition for hunting. It wasn't long before custom Contender barrels chambered in JDJ cartridges became SSK's biggest seller, and one of the most popular was the .375 JDJ, which is based on the .444 Marlin case.

This cartridge easily qualifies as a hand cannon, launching a 270-grain bullet at more than 2,100 fps. Using high-ballistic-coefficient rifle bullets, it is a flat-shooter that delivers more than 1,600 foot pounds of energy at 200 yards.

The .375 JDJ is suitable for hunting big game such as elk and moose, even Alaska's coastal brown bears. In fact, J. D. Jones has taken big game on six continents using a Contender chambered for .375 JDJ. Eventually, both CorBon and Thompson/Center introduced factory ammo for the .375 JDJ, making it a "standard" cartridge instead of being purely a wildcat.

As good as it was, the T/C Contender had one serious drawback—it was not designed for chamber pressures beyond about 48,000 CUP. So it was not suitable for most current rifle cartridges, which generate peak chamber pressures of 55,000 psi to as high as 63,000 psi.

Then in the 1990s, Thompson/Center introduced an upgraded, beefed-up version of the Contender called the Encore. The new action was fully capable of handling modern high-intensity rifle cartridges, and Thompson/Center chambered the rifle version for a wide selection of cartridges, including several magnum offerings up to .416 Rigby.

J. D. immediately saw the new action's potential and began making custom barrels for the T/C Encore, chambered for larger caliber, even more powerful cartridges than he offered for the T/C Contender.

A Trio of Behemoths

During a recent visit to J. D. in Winterville, Ohio, I had the opportunity to try out three of these behemoths, the .50 Alaskan, .458 Winchester Magnum, and .620 JDJ. All three cartridges were designed for heavy rifles used on dangerous game and had a reputation for daunting, even punishing, recoil.

I, on the other hand, would be shooting T/C Encore handguns chambered for these three cartridges. Even with bull barrels, riflescopes, and massive muzzle brakes, these handguns weighed scarcely half as much as a similarly chambered rifle. Over the years, I had developed fairly high recoil tolerance, and it was about to be tested.

▲ This is the "Big Kahuna," the Smith & Wesson Model 500 revolver chambered for the .500 S&W Magnum, which has a muzzle velocity of 1,800 fps with a 325-grain bullet and generates 2,338 foot pounds of energy. This massive five-shot revolver was designed in 2003 to regain S&W's crown as the world's most powerful production handgun. With an 8 3/8-inch barrel, the Model 500 weighs 4.75 pounds (empty).

▲ This fine pronghorn buck fell to the author's scoped .460 S&W Magnum revolver. The range was 265 yards. With a blustery 20 mph wind blowing from right to left, the author hit the buck too far back. Nevertheless, he was anchored to the spot. A follow-up shot from 125 yards was necessary to put him down for good.

After loading guns and ammo into J. D.'s luxurious pickup, we drove a few miles outside of town to a property owned by J. D.'s longtime shooting crony, Blackie Sleewa. It was an idyllic setting with grassy meadows and small patches of hardwoods on rolling hills that provided a natural backstop for Blackie's shooting range. Covered firing points overlooked target butts ranging from 50 to 300 yards in one direction. Another firing line had a shooting lane cut into the woods with targets as far away as 500 yards.

Metallic silhouettes of chickens, pigs, and rams at various ranges provided a suitable challenge for my marksmanship. Each of the three Encores had a heavy bull barrel with an integral muzzle brake. Each was topped with a Bushnell variable power pistol scope using J. D.'s distinctive three-ring T'SOB scope mounts.

First up was the .50 Alaskan. This wildcat cartridge was developed in the 1950s by Alaskan Harold Johnson. He necked up the .348 Winchester to .510 caliber for use on Alaska's coastal brown bears, the biggest of which can weigh upwards of 1,600 pounds. Factory loads are available from Buffalo Bore with 450-, 500-, and 525-grain bullets. Muzzle velocity in a rifle ranges from 1,850 fps to 2,150 fps, but will be somewhat less from the Encore. J. D.'s handloads with GI .50 BMG spitzer boat tail bullets proved very accurate in the Encore.

What about recoil? Yes, it was sharp with a good deal of muzzle flip, but after 35 to 40 rounds over sand bags, I was still intact and having a good time. The result was the same with the .458 Winchester Magnum. Of course, it used similar bullet weights at about the same velocity as the .50 Alaskan, so that shouldn't be a surprise.

Even the .620 JDJ was quite manageable. This cartridge was developed using a .577 Nitro Express case shortened to two inches and expanded to accept a .620 bullet. Loaded with a 900-grain bullet, muzzle velocity is 1,000 fps. Yes, the BATFE classifies the .620 JDJ as a "Destructive Device," which means you must submit an application to the BATFE and pay a $200 transfer tax.

After firing in the neighborhood of 100 rounds through the three Encores, I was pleased with the accuracy and impressed with their performance. I'm pretty sure that, strictly speaking, one of these Encores (or one like them chambered for another cartridge) is "the most powerful handgun in the world."

But wait! Dirty Harry wasn't talking about single-shot hunting handguns or even single-action revolvers. He was talking about a pistol or double-action revolver capable of more than one shot—one that Dirty Harry could plausibly use as a law enforcement sidearm. That's a whole 'nother thing.

Wounded Pride

The folks at Smith & Wesson sort of liked the notion that, according to *Dirty Harry*, they manufactured The Most Powerful Handgun in the World. Strictly speaking (as mentioned above), that wasn't true. Freedom Arms, a Wyoming arms maker, offered the .454 Casull, which was far more powerful than the .44 Magnum.

As the seventies progressed into the eighties, custom gunmakers such as John Linebaugh had developed the .500 Linebaugh and, a couple of years later, the .475 Linebaugh. In Minnesota, Magnum Research had developed the Desert Eagle semi-auto, which was chambered for .50 Action Express, another cartridge more powerful than the .44 Magnum.

As the nineties rolled around, J. D. Jones's massive JDJ wildcats in T/C Encores and Contenders rocked the hunting handgun world. By 1997, Sturm, Ruger chambered its double-action Super Redhawk for .454 Casull.

Smith & Wesson's Model 29 .44 Magnum was seemingly left in the dust. In the hallowed corporate halls of Smith & Wesson, it must have stung to have so many pretenders to the throne—*their* throne.

In truth, Smith & Wesson had nothing to worry about. Except for Ruger, none of these small gun makers could possibly make serious inroads into S&W's share of the marketplace. The Model 29 and its several S&W variants were selling quite nicely despite all the new competition.

But pride, even corporate pride, should not be underestimated. Smith & Wesson had something up their corporate sleeve. They were about to settle the issue once and for all.

S&W made double-action revolvers in four frame sizes: the diminutive J-frame for .22 rimfire and centerfire .38 Specials; the bigger K-frame for cartridges as powerful as the .357 Magnum; the stronger L-frame, for heavy-duty use with the .357 Magnum; and the N-frame—Dirty Harry's mighty .44 Magnum.

But that was about to change.

Herb Belin, S&W product manager, proposed a new, larger-frame revolver designed to regain the throne of the world's most powerful production handgun. It would be chambered for a new cartridge developed in partnership with Peter Pi of Cor-Bon.

The .500 S&W Magnum

After eleven months of development, the S&W Model 500 revolver built on an oversize "X"-frame and the .500 S&W Magnum cartridge were unveiled on January 9, 2003, at the 2003 SHOT Show. An enthusiastic audience of dealers, distributors, and media representatives welcomed the new revolver/cartridge combination, and orders flew in.

The stainless steel Model 500 weighs 4.75 pounds and is nearly 16 inches long with a muzzle brake on the very end of its 9-inch barrel. Its fluted, five-shot cylinder is 2.3 inches long to accommodate the 2.25-inch overall length of the .500 S&W Magnum cartridge. Designing the cylinder for five shots allows thicker chamber walls to accommodate the 60,000 psi maximum chamber pressure generated by the new cartridge.

Surprisingly, the .500 S&W Magnum with a 440-grain bullet leaving the muzzle at 1,625 fps (Cor-Bon) shows a Taylor Knockout value of 51, while the powerful .375 H&H Magnum rifle cartridge, launching a 300-grain bullet at 2,670 fps (Hornady Superformance) yields a Taylor Knockout Value of only 42. This might be a bit misleading since the .375 generates 4,748 foot pounds of energy at the muzzle against 2,580 foot pounds for the .500 Smitty, but there it is.

Smith & Wesson had regained the throne in spectacular fashion. The .500 S&W Magnum is available in bullet weights from 275 grains to 500 grains and muzzle velocities above 2,000 fps in light bullet weights and more than 1,500 fps for the heaviest bullets.

The .500 S&W Magnum has proved its worth against elephants in Africa. In one instance, well-known gun writer and handgun hunter Mark Hampton downed two elephants in quick succession—each with one shot from his S&W 500 revolver. This happened after Mark had dropped a trophy elephant only to be charged at close range by a second tusker.

On a few occasions, a double discharge has been reported with the 500 S&W revolver. Smith &

▲ The .45 Colt (left) was designed in 1872 as a black powder cartridge for the Colt Model 1873 "Peacemaker." Dick Casull and Jack Fullmer lengthened and beefed up the .45 Colt 1957 to become the .454 Casull (center), toppling the .44 Magnum as the World's Most Powerful Handgun Cartridge. Then, in 2005, Smith & Wesson lengthened the .45 Colt again to create the .460 S&W Magnum, perhaps the world's best long-range handgun hunting cartridge.

▲ A scoped Smith & Wesson revolver chambered for .460 S&W Magnum is an effective hunting combination for deer-sized game to 200 yards and beyond. The .460 Smitty launches a 220-grain Hornady polymer-tipped bullet at 2,200 fps, developing more than 2,000 ft lbs of energy at the muzzle.

Wesson investigated this phenomenon using a high-speed camera capable of 10,000 frames per second. The cause proved to be an involuntary second trigger pull, though frame flexing on rare occasions unlocks and rotates the cylinder, which seems to play a part.

A second type of double discharge from an adjacent chamber has also been reported. This was speculated to be caused by the soft cup of a pistol primer coming in contact with the recoil shield, and several suppliers of cartridge cases re-specified the .500 S&W Magnum for rifle primers, which have a harder cup than most pistol primers. Because of differences in the depth of a rifle primer cup versus a

pistol primer cup, these cases were identified with a letter "R" on the headstamp.

Firing the .500 Smitty will definitely get your attention. Smith & Wesson recommends using a firm two-hand grip, although I have found no problem with a one-hand grip if you hold it firmly and actively control muzzle flip.

Smith & Wesson originally planned to make a run of only five thousand S&W 500 revolvers; but according to Herb Belin, S&W management was astonished when orders topped fifty thousand in the first year. This led the company to offer the S&W 500 in several barrel lengths from 2.75 inches as a survival revolver to a custom hunting handgun with a 14-inch barrel and a bipod.

▲ On a foggy morning in northwest Oklahoma, I watched a 10-point whitetail buck step out into a winter wheat field, joining a smaller buck and several does. One 220-grain Hornady bullet from a .460 S&W Magnum dropped him in his tracks. The range was 108 yards.

The .460 S&W Magnum

The 500's continuing popularity led the company to develop a second cartridge for the X-frame revolver. The new cartridge, named the .460 S&W Magnum, would be a straight wall case based on the .454 Casull, but nearly a half-inch longer at 1.8 inches.

This additional length would enable it to take full advantage of the X-frame's long 2.3-inch cylinder. With the additional powder capacity and 60,000 maximum operating pressure, the new cartridge would generate amazing ballistics.

In fact, the .460 S&W Magnum can drive a Hornady 220-grain bullet to 2,200 fps making it the fastest revolver cartridge in the world. This load generates 2,149 foot pounds of energy at the muzzle and hits harder than many modern deer cartridges.

With a good scope, the 460's relatively flat trajectory makes it effective on big game well beyond 200 yards. I personally have taken a pronghorn at 265 yards with the .460. On another hunt, a nice whitetail back at 108 yards dropped instantly to the .460 as did a 350 pound feral hog at considerably closer range.

For a handgun hunter who wants to hunt deer- or elk-sized game at ranges of 200 yards or more, the .460 S&W Magnum is hard to beat. But when your game animal weighs in at a ton or more and would like to transform you into a large grease spot, you want the biggest hand cannon you can find that will keep shooting until the beast is down for the count—and that is the .500 S&W Magnum in the S&W Model 500 revolver.

III. Submachine Guns

*I*t began with the "Tommy gun," more formally known as the Thompson submachine gun. It was the brain child of then-Colonel (later Brigadier General) John T. Thompson, who had a distinguished career in the US Army Ordnance Corps that included supervising development of the 1903 Springfield rifle, leading the 1904 Thompson-LaGarde handgun lethality study, and serving as chairman of the Ordnance board that adopted the M1911 semi-auto pistol.

In 1914, war broke out in Europe, but the United States remained neutral in the conflict. Thompson, who was sympathetic to the Allied cause, anticipated a great demand for military small arms and retired from the Army to become Chief Engineer for Remington Arms Company.

In that role, he supervised construction of the Eddystone firearms manufacturing facility in Chester, Pennsylvania. That plant manufactured 1914 pattern Enfield rifles for the British army and Moisin-Nagant rifles for czarist Russia.

The Blish Patent

World War I soon evolved into protracted trench warfare, and Thompson experimented with weapons designs suitable for this vicious new form of combat. His original idea was for a full-power, semi-automatic service rifle, and he was struck by the simplicity of a delayed blowback operating system patented by Navy Commander John Bell Blish. Thompson found financial backing and formed the Auto-Ordnance Company in 1916 to develop his concept.

By late 1917, Auto-Ordnance developers had realized that the Blish operating system was not suitable for the high chamber pressure generated by a full-power rifle cartridge such as the .30-06. However, the highly effective .45 ACP pistol cartridge, with its relatively low maximum chamber pressure of 21,000 psi, was ideal for the Blish system. This led Thompson to redirect development toward a "one man, hand-held" machine gun chambered for .45 ACP and intended to be used in the ongoing trench warfare of World War I. Although design issues had been resolved by 1918, the war ended before the new weapon could be mass produced and deployed.

The First Submachine Gun

Germany had developed a similar weapon concept, the *Maschinenpistole* Bergmann MP18, which was adopted in 1918 and actually saw combat in WWI with German *Sturmtruppen*. It was first used in March 1918 with decisive effect. An interesting fact about the MP18 is that its designer was Hugo Schmeisser, whose name became synonymous (but erroneously) with the German MP-40 *Maschinenpistole* of World War II.

The Bergmann is often described as the world's first submachine gun, but this, too, is erroneous. The correct term for the MP18 is *Maschinenpistole*, which translates as "machine pistol." That is the meaning behind the "MP" prefix in MP18. That's what the Germans called it, and that is its correct designation.

The world's first submachine gun is the Thompson M1921, even though the Bergmann preceded it into production by three years. Here is why:

In 1919, the Auto-Ordnance Company had a completed design for a fully automatic weapon, but with post-war peace breaking out, the military market for such a weapon had virtually dried up. As a marketing ploy, Auto-Ordnance officially coined the term *submachine gun* to describe its new weapon. So, in 1921, the Thompson M1921 went into production as the first to bear the name submachine gun. Subsequently, *submachine gun* became a generic term describing any one-man portable, full-auto weapon chambered for a pistol cartridge. That does not diminish the fact that the Thompson M1921 was the world's *first* submachine gun.

A Legend Grows

The Thompson M1921 was priced at $200 at a time when a Ford Model T cost $400, so civilian sales were very slow. However, sales to US agencies and other governments began to trickle in. The US Postal Service was one of the first to place a small order for the M1921, followed by the US Marine Corps, which used them in several South American conflicts as well as in China. Other sales went to police, civilians, government agencies, even armies and constabularies of other countries, mainly in South and Central America.

However, it was the ratification of the Eighteenth Amendment to the Constitution of the United States in

1920 that vaulted the Thompson submachine gun into nationwide notoriety forever.

The Eighteenth Amendment outlawed the sale, production, and transportation of alcoholic beverages in the United States (Prohibition). This was followed by the Volstead Act, which provided a template to enforce the new law. Prohibition led naturally to the Roaring Twenties, and, as one writer said, "The Thompson submachine gun is what made the Twenties roar."

With Prohibition in effect, it provided an ideal climate for the rise of organized crime and the official corruption that accompanied it. In the hands of Al Capone's Chicago mobsters, the Chicago Typewriter mowed down seven members of Bugs Moran's rival gang in what is now known as the St. Valentine's Day Massacre. The Thompson also became a favorite tool of bandits such as John Dillinger, Machine Gun Kelly, and Bonnie and Clyde.

In January 1934, Dillinger and members of his gang were captured in Tucson, Arizona, after a hotel fire. A witness recognized one of the gang members and notified police who captured Dillinger and others in a series of raids. Two Thompson M1921s that belonged to Dillinger and were captured in the raids are still on display at Tucson Police Headquarters. A third Dillinger Thompson, also captured in the Tucson raids, is on display at FBI headquarters in Washington, D.C.

▼ These two Thompson submachine guns are on display at the Tucson Police Department Headquarters building in Tucson, Arizona. The two submachine guns, along with a third, belonged to Public Enemy Number One, John Dillinger, when he and his gang were arrested by law enforcement officers in Tucson on January 25, 1934. The third Thompson from the raid is on display at the FBI museum in Washington, DC.

▲ The simplified military version of the Tommy Gun, named the M1, and the even more simplified M1A1 were considerably cheaper and faster to produce to meet wartime demands during World War II. *Photo credit: Bill Ball*

In 1928, Auto-Ordnance modified the M1921 and re-designated it as the Model 1928. This was the first Thompson submachine gun that came into wide use by the military. Both the US Navy and Marines bought considerable quantities throughout the 1930s. In addition, lend-lease Thompson M1928s were produced for China, France, and the United Kingdom.

A variation, the M1928A1, was notable mainly for its horizontal forearm, replacing the distinctive raked pistol grip of earlier Thompson sub guns. It also had provisions for a military-type sling.

In April 1942, the Army adopted a simplified Thompson sub gun dubbed the M1. This new Tommy gun had a simple blowback action, eliminating the Blish lock of earlier Thompson sub guns. Also eliminated was the provision for attaching a drum magazine and the cooling fins on the barrel. The charging handle was moved to the right side of the receiver and a simplified L-shaped, two-position rear sight replaced the earlier flip-up adjustable Lyman sight.

A further simplified military Thompson, the M1A1, was adopted a few months later in October 1942. This new variation eliminated the hammer and floating firing pin. This was replaced by a fixed firing pin machined onto the bolt face.

Although the M1 and M1A1 were produced at only a fraction of the cost of earlier Thompsons, the Army adopted the even less expensive M3 and M3A1 "grease gun" to replace the Thompson. However, production delays and modifications prevented large-scale replacement, and the government continued to purchase Thompsons until early 1944.

Following World War II, Thompson sub guns continued to be a familiar sight on new battlefields throughout Europe, Asia, and elsewhere—often on both sides of a conflict.

In combat, most troops liked the Thompson, but inevitably there were some knocks, too. At more than a pound heavier than the M1 Garand service rifle, the Thompson received many complaints of excessive weight. Other users realized that the Thompson's weight made full-auto fire more controllable. Weight also made the Thompson more stable for accurate, aimed fire.

Also receiving complaints was the M1928A1 Thompson's 50-round drum magazine. Despite its formidable firepower, troops complained that it was too heavy, tricky, and slow to reload, unwieldy in heavy jungle or brush, easily damaged under field combat conditions, and it rattled whenever you moved the gun. Much more popular were the 20- and 30-round "stick" magazines that also were standard issue.

Total wartime production was about 1.7 million with nearly 1.4 million being M1s and M1A1s. The remainder were M1928s and M1928A1s. Total worldwide production from 1921 to the present, including all variants, is pegged at 2.7 million.

Today, collectors can pay $15,000 to $30,000 for a Thompson, depending on condition and scarcity of a particular model. One Thompson was reputed to have been owned by Bonnie and Clyde, but without documentation. It sold at auction recently for $130,000. The two Dillinger Thompsons on display in Tucson have iron-clad provenance to the legendary outlaw. We can only speculate how much either might bring on the auction block.

I have had a couple of opportunities to fire a Tommy gun. The first time I fired one, I was surprised how easy it was to control if I leaned into it as I pulled the trigger. It bucked gently against my shoulder, and I hardly noticed it because my attention was drawn to the loud, staccato *pop-pop-pop* and the .45 ACP GI hardball impacting on a row of water-filled gallon jugs that burst in a drenching spray as they were flung off

▼ The author fires a Model 1928A1 Thompson submachine gun. Note the Cutts Compensator on the muzzle and the 30-round stick magazine, which WWII combat troops preferred over an unwieldy drum magazine. First offered for sale in 1921, the Tommy Gun became a symbol of the Prohibition-era and was widely used during WWII. This legendary weapon is the author's favorite sub-gun.

▲ The author examines gunsmith Lon Laufman's German MP-40, which has its folding stock in the stowed position. The photo shows the inadequate hand grip/mag well. With bullets flying, a soldier often mistakenly gripped the magazine, which often caused a stoppage. Grabbing the slender—and probably hot—barrel was not an option!

their two-by-four perch. That was fun best described as *YEE-HAH*!

Although I can never afford to own a Tommy gun at the price it commands today, it remains one of my favorite firearms of all time. If I could own one, my first choice would be a Model 1921, the original Chicago Typewriter. Second would be a Model 1928A1. A guy can always dream, can't he?

The onset of World War II spurred the seemingly overnight development of new submachine guns, a trend that continues even today. Here are a few of the best:

German MP-40

Erroneously called a *Schmeisser* by Allied troops, the German MP-40 was actually designed by Berthold Geipel of Erma Werke. Hugo Schmeisser designed the MP18/I, which saw service in World War I, but he did not design the MP-40. Adopted by the German Army in 1940, the MP-40 was issued mainly to the *Fallschirmjäger* (paratroops), as well as infantry platoon and squad leaders.

This policy changed after the Battle of Stalingrad, where massed formations of Soviet Army troops armed with PPSh-41 submachine guns outgunned German forces in close-range urban combat. By the end of the war, platoon-sized Wehrmacht units on the Western Front were armed with MP-40s.

Unfortunately for the German Army, the MP-40 had some serious ergonomic drawbacks. One of them was its 10-inch-long unsleeved barrel. It didn't take long for the barrel to become blistering hot in a firefight. This was a serious burn hazard and a distraction to a soldier trying to take cover in close combat.

Another ergonomic flaw was the MP-40's inadequate hand grip just aft of the magazine well. The magazine itself was a natural fore grip. Unfortunately, any side pressure from the shooter's hand on the magazine tended to misalign the magazine's feed lips, causing failure-to-feed stoppages.

That being said, the MP-40's menacing appearance and wartime history give it an evil mystique that makes it very popular with weapons collectors.

Russian PPSh-41

Before the AK-47, another weapon symbolized the post-war Communist military threat leading to the Cold War—the PPSh-41 submachine gun, sometimes

▲ Mike Venturino fires the German MP-40. His support hand correctly holds the MP-40's rather inadequate handgrip/magazine well instead of grabbing the magazine itself. Holding the magazine can misalign the feed lips and cause a failure-to-feed malfunction.
Photo credit: Yvonne Venturino

▲ The Soviet PPSh-41 was chambered for a relatively small caliber pistol cartridge, the 7.62x25mm Tokarev and had a rate of fire above 1,000 rpm. It could empty a 35-round magazine such as the one on gunwriter Mike Venturino's PPSh-41 in just under two seconds.
Photo credit: Yvonne Venturino

▲ Tyler Hartung fires a PPSh-41 at a fund-raising shoot near Tucson, Arizona. The weapon's 1,000-plus rpm rate of fire produced a distinctive ripping *BRRRRP* that gave it the nickname Burp Gun.

called the Burp Gun. PPSh stood for *Pistolet-Pulemyot Shpagina*, or Shpagina machine pistol, which was developed by Soviet designer Georgi Shpagin. It was a selective-fire, open-bolt, blowback submachine gun made mostly of stamped steel parts and chambered for the 7.62x25mm Tokarev pistol cartridge.

Dimensions of this cartridge were virtually identical to, but slightly more powerful than, the 7.63x25mm Mauser pistol cartridge.

Manufactured with a fixed wooden stock, the PPSh-41 had a high cyclic rate of about 1,000 to 1,200 rpm and ejected from the top. Equipped with a crude, flip-up rear sight, it weighed about 12 pounds with a fully-loaded 71-round drum magazine and around 9.5 pounds with a loaded 35-round box magazine. It had no foregrip, and the shooter usually held the magazine with the support hand.

The drum magazine proved to be fragile and therefore unreliable under field conditions. It was also slow to load and expensive to produce. The Soviets introduced a modified drum magazine made of thicker metal late in the war, but soon replaced it with a more reliable 35-round box magazine.

Red Army troops used the PPSh-41 with devastating effect in the Battle of Stalingrad and subsequent engagements on the Red Army's march to a final showdown with the Wehrmacht in Berlin.

By the end of WWII, more than six million PPSh-41s had been produced, and the Soviet Union began distributing it to Communist regimes and guerrilla forces worldwide.

This included North Korea and Red China, and both countries produced slightly modified copies of the PPSh-41 under license. This must have caused substantial logistical problems during the Korean War because the North Korean Type 49 used only drum magazines and the Chinese Type 50 used only box magazines.

Dubbed the Burp Gun, the PPSh-41 was a fearsome weapon as hordes of howling Communist troops charged grim and determined UN soldiers amid the shrill blare of Chinese bugles. In night patrolling operations, the fighting was usually close and vicious; and the 1,000 rpm firepower of the PPSh-41 was often the decisive factor.

I recently had the opportunity to try the PPSh-41 at a shooting range in Ohio. We had numerous stoppages that we attributed to the relatively anemic 7.63x25mm Mauser ammo we had on hand. Still, I was able to briefly experience the ripping *BRRRRP* that gave the burp gun its nickname.

M3 Grease Gun

Adopted by the US Army in December 1942, the United States Submachine Gun, M3 was intended to replace the Thompson M1 and M1A1 submachine guns. Called the Grease Gun because it resembled a common automotive lubricating device, the M3 was about 2.6 pounds lighter than the Thompson, and it was much cheaper to produce.

Like the Thompson, the M3 was chambered for the powerful .45 ACP cartridge, but it had a much slower rate of fire at 450 rpm compared to the Thompson's 600 rpm (even higher in some models). Some critics regard this as a serious drawback, but with about 7.5 rounds per second spewing out of its muzzle, it could empty a 30-round magazine in 4 seconds. That should keep most folks' heads down. The slower cyclic rate also makes controlled three- to four-round bursts much easier to manage.

When the first M3s reached combat zones, complaints rolled in regarding a variety of problems with the new sub gun. The Army addressed this with a series of modifications that were incorporated into the M3 in December 1944 and which became the M3A1. Despite the improvements, a few complaints of accidental discharges persisted through the Korean War. These mainly involved dropping the weapon onto a hard surface with the bolt forward. A hard impact might jar the bolt back far enough to feed a round, but not engage the sear. Then with the cartridge chambered, the bolt would close, firing the round.

By the end of the war, combined production of the M3 and M3A1 submachine guns totaled a little more than 620,000 units. By comparison, wartime production of the Thompson M1 and M1A1 came to more than 1.5 million by the time production ceased in February 1944.

At the end of the war, the Army completed the phasing-out of the Thompson M1/M1A1 in favor of the M3/M3A1 Grease Gun. It remained in service until 1992. A fair number of M3 and M3A1 Grease Guns are in civilian hands and are available for Class III NFA transfer. However, its main significance is that it

▲ The Soviet PPS 43 was designed as a compact, low-cost alternative to the PPSh-41. It required only one-third the machining time and less than half the raw steel needed to produce a PPSh-41. It also had a much lower 600 to 900 rpm rate of fire. This lower rate was still combat effective while conserving ammo.

▲ Intended to replace the Thompson submachine gun, the M3 (and later M3A1) Grease Gun used mostly stamped and welded steel parts. It was much cheaper to produce than the Thompson, but saw limited use during WWII. After the war the M3A1 became standard issue. Although it was officially withdrawn from US military service in 1957, it was used both in Korea and Vietnam. The M3A1 was even issued to a few armored vehicle crews in the 1991 Gulf War.
Photo credit: Bill Ball

▲ Although the slide is marked as a Model 17, the detachable shoulder stock and select-fire switch on the rear of the slide near the author's thumb show that it is actually a Glock 18 selective-fire machine pistol. The Model 18 can take up to a 33-round magazine and is chambered for 9x19mm Parabellum. *Photo credit: Bill Ball*

replaced the Thompson M1/M1A in US Army service. Otherwise, I see it as one of the least desirable Class III weapons that are legal for civilian ownership.

Uzi

A few years after World War II, a new submachine gun appeared that would become an indelible presence among military small arms. That sub gun is, of course, the Uzi.

Named for its creator, Major Uziel Gal of the Israeli Defense Forces, the Uzi was designed in 1948 and adopted by the IDF in 1954. Early models had a removable wooden stock, which added nearly a foot to its length, masking one of the Uzi's most important innovations, its compact design. Later, folding stock versions took full advantage of this feature. As a result, the 10-inch-barreled, folding stock Uzi was 6.5 inches shorter than the German MP-40, which also had a 10-inch barrel.

This compactness was possible because of the Uzi's telescoping bolt, which nested much of the Uzi's barrel within the bolt. Aside from being more compact, the telescoping bolt also moved the axis of recoil farther to the rear, just in front of the pistol grip. This reduced muzzle flip, making full-auto fire significantly more controllable.

A second major innovation was the magazine housed in the pistol grip. Although this feature had been used in semi-auto pistols since 1893 (in the Borchhardt C93), virtually all previous submachine gun designs located the magazine forward of the trigger guard. Although housing the magazine in the pistol grip might not seem like an important innovation, it in fact gave the shooter a small, but important edge in close quarters combat. To survive in CQB, a combatant must maintain a 360-degree scan to assess possible threats in the immediate area. Using an ergonomics factor sometimes called "hand finds hand," a combatant can remove a spent magazine and insert a fresh one without having to look down and interrupt his scan. This also allows effortless reloads in night combat conditions.

At about 7.7 pounds without a loaded magazine, the Uzi was lighter than most contemporary submachine guns. Two variants, the mini-Uzi and micro-Uzi, are smaller and more compact, but never gained the popularity of the original Uzi.

More modern sub guns, such as the Heckler & Koch MP5 are significantly lighter than the Uzi and may have other improvements such as upgraded sights. Nevertheless, a combatant equipped with the sixty-five-year-old Uzi can consider himself as well-armed as any adversary.

The Uzi is a personal favorite of mine, especially since conversion kits are available to allow it to use the .45 ACP cartridge instead of the less powerful 9x19mm Parabellum.

H&K MP5

Developed in the 1960s by Heckler & Koch, the MP5 quickly gained widespread popularity among special operations, personal security, and law enforcement personnel. The MP5 is a select-fire, delayed blowback weapon that operates from a closed bolt. It is chambered for 9x19mm *Parabellum* and weighs 6.8 pounds in the MP5A3 retractable stock version.

More than ten countries currently manufacture the MP5 under license, and not surprisingly, about one hundred variants exist with various combinations of retractable stocks; different barrel lengths; full-auto, semi-auto or three-round burst triggers, etc.

It is obviously a fine military and law enforcement weapon, and a few have found their way into civilian hands. But for my money, I'd rather own any of the sub guns in this chapter—except perhaps for the M3 Grease Gun.

Numerous other sub guns have emerged since World War II, more than I can adequately describe here. But, in my opinion, the examples in this chapter are especially noteworthy, and each occupies a unique niche in the history of submachine guns.

IV. Tricked-out .22s

For more than a century, an American kid's first "real" gun was usually a .22 caliber rifle. In the Depression years and earlier, it might have been a .22 Short, .22 BB Cap, or other variation, but the hands-down all-time favorite chambering was (and is) the .22 Long Rifle cartridge.

Then and now, responsible parents made sure their son or daughter understood the grave responsibility of owning, carrying, and using what is most surely a lethal weapon. It was a solemn rite of passage to entrust a young person with such power. A parent or close relative delivered careful instruction on safe gun handling, marksmanship and maintaining a firearm—along with stern warnings about the consequences of failing to live up to that trust.

Under close supervision, we learned sight picture, trigger squeeze, and all the other elements necessary to deliver a well-aimed shot into a target. As adults, we instilled these time-honored principles in our own children and the tradition endures.

Most of us have never forgotten those early lessons and that first rifle. Nor have we forgotten the .22 Long Rifle—the cartridge that made that first rifle "a real gun." Now, as adults, we still like to have good, accurate .22s available to plink or hunt small game.

Our local gun stores have many fine, accurate .22 rifles we can choose from—bolt-action, pump action, lever action, semi-auto, whatever. We can hunt with them, shoot holes in paper, or make tin cans dance at will, but for some of us, that's not enough.

A Dark Desire

Somewhere, in the dark recesses of our hearts lies a yearning—an urge long-suppressed, but never quite forgotten—a desire to forget all that junk about sight picture, breath control, and trigger squeeze—just snatch up a full-auto machine gun with a high-cap magazine and *let 'er rip!*

We'd grin gleefully as water-filled jugs and balloons burst and danced, water spraying in all directions. Then, with magazine spent, muzzle smoking, and fist pumping in the air, we'd let out a triumphant yell worthy of the Stonewall Brigade or Joshua Chamberlain's 20th Maine (for you Yankees).

The fact is that a whole industry has emerged to build .22 caliber firearms that cater to we who harbor this unrepentant lust. Only a few of these would qualify as full-auto, nevertheless, they all, in one way or another, feed our need to *let 'er rip!*

The Ruger 10/22

The introduction of the Ruger 10/22 carbine in 1964 was the trigger that spurred us on. This innovative, but simple semi-auto was equipped with a removable, 10-round rotary magazine and a unique method of attaching the barrel that makes installation and removal extremely easy with no need for a gunsmith to perform the chore.

You could install a match-grade bull barrel, you could have a synthetic, fancy walnut or a colorful, laminated, thumbhole stock. You could trick it out with a military-style folding stock and a hi-cap magazine holding fifty rounds or more.

You could spring for a bundle of cash to have a complete custom 10/22 built by a custom arms maker such as Clark Custom Guns or Power.

Gatling gun?

Which brings me to the SaBer Two-22 "Gatling Gun" by Omega Performance Products of Carson City, Nevada. When I first saw its photo on the Internet, I was captivated. Sporting a side-mounted hand crank, it squatted low on its sturdy tripod, its twin barrels surrounded by perforated barrel shrouds and topped with high antiaircraft-style sights. It looked menacing and deadly.

It was beautiful, and my long-secret desire began to emerge—*big time!*

The SaBer Two-22 is actually a CAD-designed and CNC-machined kit made from 6061-T6 aluminum. This ingenious device transforms a pair of .22 rimfire Ruger 10/22 barreled actions into a twin-barreled shootin' iron that can put out an impressive, machine-gun-like burst of fire.

I say *machine-gun-like* because—legally—the SaBer Two-22 is not fully-automatic. Therefore, it is not a *machine gun*. As defined by the federal government, a full-automatic firearm is one that discharges more than once with a single pull of the trigger. Instead, the

▲ Using a pair of Ruger 10-22 barreled actions, the SaBer Two-22 "Gatling Gun" by Omega Performance Products offers simulated machine gun fire as fast as you can turn the crank. It is not true full-auto because each shot is fired from a separate pull of the trigger. The SaBer Two-22 does not use revolving barrels and more closely resembles a Gardner gun (see chapter 9).

SaBer Two-22 uses a pivoting cam bar to engage the triggers of the two barreled actions alternately.

Truthfully, the SaBer Two-22 is not a gatling gun, either. Its two barrels do not rotate. They are fixed and fire alternately via the hand-cranked cam bar. Its function more closely resembles the Gardner gun, an early rival of the Gatling gun which also fired two barrels alternately.

The hand-cranked SaBer Two-22 spits out four .22 Long Rifle bullets with every full turn of the handle. Using two 25- or 50-round magazines, the SaBer Two-22 is capable of a cyclic rate exceeding 200 rounds per minute. The limiting factor is how fast you can turn the hand crank while holding the cam bar trigger back.

As I unpacked my SaBer Two-22 kit, I could see that assembly would take the best part of an afternoon. The component parts were precision machined from aircraft-quality aluminum, just as advertised, and the main frame was pre-assembled

with the trigger cam bar, pistol grip, and tripod mounting plate with pintle pin. Between the cam and the frame was a wafer-thin thrust bearing to minimize friction as the cam alternately trips the pair of 10/22 triggers. The folding tripod with pivoting feet was also fully assembled.

The remaining parts were an aluminum receiver cover, two perforated barrel shrouds, anti-aircraft-type sights, hand crank, barrel clamp, and a pin set to replace existing pins in the two Ruger10/22 barreled actions that provide the guts for this project.

I removed the two barreled actions from their gunstocks and placed them so the top of the receivers faced each other. The next step was to replace the flush pins in the two receivers with round head pins. Without the gunstock to keep them in place, the flush pins could fall out under recoil vibration. However, the replacement round head pins solve the problem neatly.

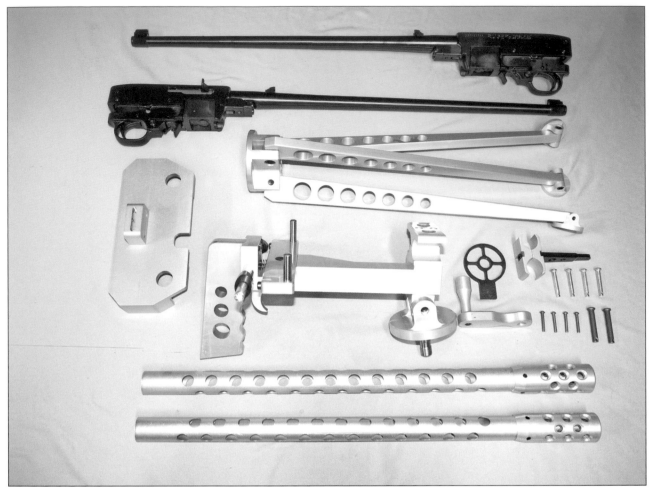

▲ You provide two Ruger 10-22 barreled actions and the SaBer Two-22 kit provides the rest. No special tools are required to assemble the gun, but fine-tuning the trigger pulls is necessary to achieve reliable functioning.

Except for the last step, the remaining assembly was easily accomplished, and my SaBer Two-22 had assumed its menacing posture atop its tripod. But it was not quite ready to take to the range. The stumbling block was trigger timing.

The Trigger Disconnector

The problem was the trigger disconnector. A semi-automatic firearm has a trigger disconnector that prevents full-auto fire by making it necessary to release the trigger to fire the next shot. On the SaBer Two-22, this means the trigger cam must press each (of the two) triggers far enough to fire the shot then release it to disengage the disconnector. To accomplish this feat, the two barreled actions must be positioned very carefully and clamped in place on the frame so both will fire continuously.

I soon found out this is harder than it sounds. I spent more than an hour clamping, dry-fire testing, loosening the clamp, inching one action or the other forward or back, reclamping, dry-fire testing—and repeat. Eventually, I got it right, and it was time to go to the range.

But first, we needed to obtain suitable high capacity magazines for the SaBer Two-22. Obviously, the standard Ruger 10-round rotary magazine doesn't have sufficient capacity to make a "machine gun" sing. More—much more—is needed.

After-market brands offer a variety of 50-round drum and "tear drop" magazines that provide the capacity. Fifty-round drums look pretty cool hanging on each side of the SaBer Two-22, but negative reviews on the Internet indicated a tendency toward feeding malfunctions. The MWG 50-round teardrop magazine offered by Brownell's seemed to offer better reliability, so I ordered four to use with my SaBer Two-22.

These 50-round teardrop magazines are made of a durable transparent plastic that makes it easy to see

▲ Tyler Hartung prepares to fire the SaBer Two-22 at a county-owned range near Tucson, Arizona.

how many rounds remain in the magazine. Loading them, however, is more complicated than simply pushing rounds past the feed lips.

Instead, you must remove the back cover, retrieve a spring key conveniently stored inside, wind the spring enough to load the first five rounds onto the flexible belt, release the spring, load forty more onto the belt, wind the spring the rest of the way, and hold it while you load the last five rounds, release the spring, put the spring key away, and replace the back cover. *Whew!* It makes me tired just to think about it.

Nevertheless, I repeated the process with three more teardrop magazines and headed to a nearby shooting range ready to rock and roll.

The range we used had concrete benches and target butts at various ranges from 5 to 100 yards. It was a public range, and it wasn't long before a small crowd assembled to watch us set up our SaBer Two-22. When we had it ready, charged the chambers, and started cranking.

Smiles erupted among our onlookers as the stuttering reports rang out and holes began to speckle the target face. To start out, we had placed the target at 10 yards, and the pattern was about 2 feet wide. Clearly, the gun and its anti-aircraft-style sights were not a precision combination.

A determined tinkerer might, with a lot of effort, improve the SaBer Two-22's accuracy, but barring that

▲ With two 50-round teardrop magazines from Brownell's in place, the SaBer Two-22 is ready to rip. However, the target, fired at 10 yards, reveals that it might roll a tin can at that range, but it's a plinker, at best.

it is just a toy—but a *fun* toy. So, we spent an hour or so making noise and emptying rimfire cases.

However, the novelty soon wore off, and it was time to break 'er down and head for the house.

A Real .22 Gatling Gun

The semi-annual Big Sandy Machine Gun Shoot is a good candidate for anybody's bucket list. On its quarter-mile-long firing line, you are likely to see almost every machine gun ever actually manufactured. When I attended the October 2012 shoot, I saw a beautiful, hand-made .22 Gatling gun.

It was mounted on a wheeled hardwood field carriage, and a pivoting lever provided rudimentary elevation and traversing capability. Its six steel barrels and polished brass breech shroud gleamed in the Arizona sun as its builder, Bill Tjerrild of Klamath Falls, Oregon, and his assistant struggled to make its American 180 pan magazine (described below) feed properly. As I watched them, I began to realize that enjoying a sweet little toy like this is a lot more complicated than loading a magazine and turning the crank to spit out a torrent of .22 rounds. You also needed to be capable of troubleshooting a problem in the field and repairing it on-site. In this case, the problem seemed to be more complicated than my problem with the SaBer Two-22's trigger disconnectors.

▲ The Tjerrild .22 caliber Gatling field gun takes its place proudly on the firing line at the Big Sandy Machine Gun Shoot near Wikieup, Arizona. Note the polished brass, high capacity, horizontal pan magazine.

As time wore on, it became apparent I would not get to see them shoot the little Gatling, so I moved on to see what else was on the firing line.

As luck would have it, one of the most interesting .22s ever made was being put through its paces at the next firing point.

The Ultimate Tricked-out .22?

Perhaps the ultimate tricked-out .22 is a little number that looks like the result of mating a Thompson submachine gun with a Lewis gun. It is, of course, the American 180 I saw at the Big Sandy Machine gun Shoot.

Although it is classified as a submachine gun, the American 180 stretches that definition to the limits.

Instead of being chambered for a centerfire pistol round, such as the 9mm Parabellum or .45 ACP, the American 180 is chambered for the diminutive .22 Long Rifle. Early production used a steel drum (or pan) magazine containing 177 rounds in three layers, facing inward. It was mounted horizontally on top of the receiver similar to a WWI Lewis Gun. More recent models used a polymer magazine that held as many as 275 rounds.

Arms designer Dick Casull patented the American 180 in the mid 1960s, and its high (1,200 rpm) cyclic rate and an optional laser sight soon caused quite a stir. A video clip that showed an American 180 reducing a concrete block wall to rubble impressed many shooters.

▲ Bill Tjerrild, who built this handmade .22 Gatling gun, and his assistant troubleshoot a feeding problem with the American 180-type magazine the little Gatling uses. Such are the joys and tears associated with complex mechanical toys.

Also impressive was a report that a prison riot came to a screeching halt when guards "painted" the ringleaders with a laser mounted on their American 180s.

At Big Sandy, I watched a shooter fire his American 180. Its rapid song seemed strangely gentle against the staccato roar of heavy machine guns and the occasional deeper note of .50 BMG M2s in the background. Given the current prices of .22 Long Rifle ammo, it seemed fortunate that the American 180's ammo appetite is fed by a drum magazine.

At the current gun show price of .22 Long rifle ammo (mid-2013), the American 180's cyclic rate would chew through ammo to the tune of about $240 per minute (1,200 rounds per minute). The capacity of the

American 180's original drums is 177 rounds and loading it is slow and laborious.

Emptying an American 180 drum is another matter entirely.

A full-auto burst would take merely nine seconds and $35 to bleed a drum dry. That's about the same as a good steak and cocktail or eighteen holes at a decent golf course. As a lifelong friend of mine used to say, "You pays your money and you takes your choice."

Can Full-Auto Be Cute?

Not so many years ago, a small family-owned company made half-scale, full-auto replicas of Browning machine guns chambered in .22 Long Rifle and .22 Winchester

▲ Looking like a cross between a Lewis gun and a Tommy Gun, the American 180 rips off a long burst at the Big Sandy Shoot in Arizona. Its 1,200 rpm rate of fire burns up scarce .22 long rifle ammo at an alarming rate.

▼ Lakeside Machine LLC, which recently closed its doors, manufactured miniature semi-auto replicas of the Browning Model 1919a4 machine gun. However, at this writing, two of these well-made little gems are still available for sale. Also for sale is a similar replica Browning Model 1917a1, complete with water jacketed barrel. If you need to ask "How much?" you probably can't afford one. I wish I could. . . .

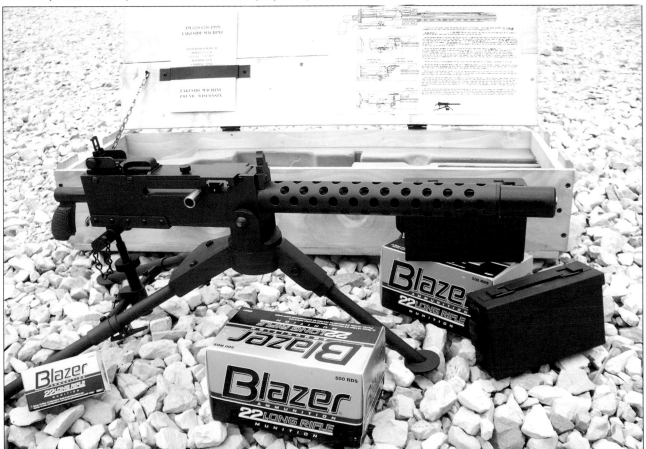

▲ Just what every AR-15/M-16 owner needs is a belt-fed .22 long rifle upper receiver, such as this one from Lakeside Machine, LLC. Called the Razorback, the upper is compatible with a full-auto M16 lower. A semi-auto version is available for AR-15 owners

Magnum. This included Model 1919s and 1917s in .22 LR. and the (not so) mighty M2 in .22 Magnum.

In 1986, with enactment of a federal ban on sale of newly-manufactured machine guns to civilians, this company, Tippman, stopped manufacturing these replicas and turned to manufacturing paint-ball guns. Today, the Tippman miniature machine guns are collector's items commanding premium prices.

For those who want one of these gems, prospects are dim, as they don't often surface for sale. Still, there's a glimmer of hope because a small Arkansas company has taken up the banner—sort of.

Lakeside Machine, LLC in Horseshoe Bend, Arkansas, makes a semi-auto version of the Browning M1919

and a proprietary design called the Razorback, which is a belt-fed semi-auto .22 Long Rifle upper for an M16 or AR 15 lower. That's the good news. Now here is the bad news. Lakeside Machine will make only one more run of M1919s and one run of Razorbacks before they close their doors for good on December 31, 2013. Lakeside is taking reservations to buy one of these unique tricked-out 22s, and I am putting my name on the list.

So, by the time you read these words, Lakeside will be a thing of the past. According to owner and operator Eric Graetz, it's time to retire, but he's willing to sell his business if an interested buyer presents himself. We can hope.

V. ARs, AKs, et al

For more than fifty years, the M-16, the AK-47, and their variants have faced each other across bloody battlefields on at least four continents. Here in the United States, the face-off continues even if the battles don't shed blood—at least not very much.

We have two (armed) camps, one honors the genius of a Russian World War II tank commander named Mikhail Kalashnikov. The other pays homage to a lesser well-known American arms designer, the late Eugene Stoner.

Both the AK-47 and the M-16 are true assault rifles. That is, both rifles are select-fire military weapons capable of full-automatic fire as well as semi-auto fire. Semi-auto only versions sold in the civilian market are *not* assault rifles, no matter what they are called by the sensation-seeking media. The shooting industry has taken to calling these semi-auto models *modern sporting rifles*, a euphemism intended to sound less threatening to non-shooters. I personally prefer to call them "tactical sporting rifles," which I believe more correctly states their function.

Kalashnikov's Brain Child

Although other assault rifle designs have been produced in various countries since the 1960s, the Kalashnikov AK-47 and the M-16 are by far the most widely used military small arms worldwide. AK-47, of course, ranks first and the M-16 a distant second.

This is partly because the AK-47 was the standard issue infantry weapon of most Warsaw Pact nations as well as the Soviet Union. The major reason, however, is

▲ Garry James's AK-47 is in excellent condition with blemish-free metal work and well-finished stock and forend.

that the Soviet Union had a strategy of supporting armed revolution around the world to achieve their expansionist goals. As a result, the USSR supplied millions of cheaply produced AK-47s to insurgent forces on every inhabited continent (except, possibly, North America).

In the hands of these guerrilla fighters, the AK-47 became a universal symbol of revolution. In at least one case, successful revolutionaries designed a new national flag bearing the distinctive profile of an AK-47 to commemorate its role in achieving victory.

The AK-47 is a second generation assault rifle that borrows proven features from earlier designs, especially the German *Sturmgewehr* MP-44. Aside from the borrowed general design concept, Kalashnikov chambered the AK-47 for the 7.62x39mm, an intermediate cartridge similar to the 7.92x33mm Kurz used in the German MP-44.

The new cartridge would be loaded into a distinctive damage-resistant, 30-round, "banana" magazine, which provided smooth feeding in full-auto fire.

Early production runs used a stamped and welded sheet metal receiver, but were plagued by a high rejection rate. The problem was solved by substituting a higher cost, machined receiver. In 1959, a redesigned sheet metal receiver was introduced along with several other improvements, including a slanted muzzle brake that counteracted muzzle rise under recoil. It was also about a third lighter than the original AK-47. The new variation was redesignated the AKM (modernized or upgraded).

This gave the Soviets a reliable and simple infantry weapon that a conscript soldier could use and maintain with minimal training. It was not especially accurate, capable only of 4- to 6-inch groups at 100 yards. Nevertheless, it was considered good enough to be an effective infantry weapon.

The much-evolved AKM was an excellent example of a "mature" technology. In a few short years, it would be pitted against an enemy armed with an infantry weapon that was a perfect example of new, emerging technology. This new rifle discarded traditional notions of what a military rifle should be—or even look like.

Stoner's Brain Child

A couple of facts about the AR-15/M-16 are often overlooked. First, Eugene Stoner did not design the AR-15. Second, the AR-15 does not use a "direct impingement" operating system. I'd bet those two statements captured most readers' attention, so I'd better explain.

Eugene Stoner is often regarded as one of America's greatest arms designers. His designs go well beyond his accomplishment that resulted in the AR-15. Wait, did that sound as if I just contradicted what I said in the last paragraph?

If that's what you think, you'd be wrong.

Stoner and the AR-10

In 1955, Eugene Stoner designed a ground-breaking new battle rifle called the AR-10. This rifle was chambered for the new NATO standard cartridge, the 7.62x51mm NATO. This rifle featured a phenolic resin buttstock and forend along with an aluminum receiver that made the rifle roughly a full pound lighter than contemporary autoloading military rifles.

The buttstock was in line with the barrel, which minimized any tendency toward muzzle climb when the rifle was fired, especially in full-auto. It also employed a patented new operating system (which I'll get to a bit later).

At the time, the US Army was seeking a replacement for the aging M-1 Garand. Several rifles had been submitted for testing, including an entry from *Fabrique Nationale* designated T-48 (now known as the FAL) and an entry from Springfield Armory called the T-44 (now known as the M-14). The AR-10 was a late entry into the competition, and it reportedly outperformed the other entries in every category. Despite this fact, Army evaluators chose the T-44, partly because the AR-10's radical design did not resemble then-current notions of what a service rifle should look like and partly because of failure of a composite aluminum/steel barrel during testing.

Now, back to the original statement: Eugene Stoner did not design the AR-15.

At the request of the US Army, ArmaLite assigned Stoner's chief assistant Robert Fremont and Jim Sullivan to scale-down the AR-10, and the result was the AR-15. The new rifle was to be chambered a high-velocity .22 caliber cartridge that could meet Army requirements to be able to penetrate both sides of a G.I. helmet at 500 yards and remain supersonic at that range. The new cartridge also had to demonstrate lethality equal to or better than the .30 Carbine cartridge.

Fremont and Sullivan Deserve Much of the Credit

To sum it up, Eugene Stoner in his role as chief designer for Armalite designed the AR-10 battle rifle, which used a new operating system patented by Stoner. It was Fremont and Sullivan who designed the AR-15 by scaling down and modifying the AR-10 design to shoot the newly introduced .222 Magnum.

Direct Impingement, Or No?

The first direct impingement operating system appeared in 1901 on an experimental rifle, the Rossignol B1, and subsequent B2 through B5 models. The most successful direct impingement rifle was the MAS 40 adopted by the French army in March 1940. A Swedish rifle, the Ag m/42, also used a direct impingement system.

However, according to Eugene Stoner himself, the AR-15's operating system is an "expanding gas" system, not direct impingement. Quoting from Stoner's US Patent No. 2,951,242:

"This invention is a true expanding gas system instead of the conventional impinging gas system. By utilization of a metered amount of gas from the barrel, the automatic rifle mechanism is less sensitive to different firing pressures caused by variations in the propelling charge."

The difference is subtle. According to Stoner, because the tube that transports combustion gas from a port in the barrel delivers it into a hollow tube *perched as an appendage* on top of the bolt carrier, this does not impinge directly onto either the bolt or the bolt carrier. Instead, it transforms the bolt carrier into a gas piston that unlocks and transports the bolt to the rear to extract the empty brass. Then, on the forward stroke, the bolt strips a fresh round from the magazine, chambers it and rotates to engage the locking lugs.

As mentioned before, this is a subtle distinction, but Stoner's patent is based on this distinction, and the US Patent Office (USPTO) agrees. By issuing a patent to Stoner, the USPTO declares the Stoner mechanism to be a "novel invention" different and distinct from all previous self-loading firearm operating systems.

Scaled Down for a Small Cartridge

The popular .222 Remington cartridge was an obvious choice for the new AR-15, but early testing revealed that it could not meet the Army specifications stated above. So, Armalite found it necessary to design a new, higher velocity cartridge to deliver the necessary performance.

Working with Remington engineers, they lengthened the .222 Remington case and shortened the neck, which increased powder capacity about 20 percent with a corresponding increase in muzzle velocity. Remington introduced this new cartridge as the .222 Remington Magnum, which quickly achieved popularity among varmint hunters. But then, fate and the US Army intervened, and sales of the .222 Remington Magnum shriveled and died.

The .222 Rem Mag easily met the Army requirements, but in the grand old Army tradition, engineers changed the angle of the shoulder for more reliable feeding and shortened the neck. The result was the 5.56 x 45mm cartridge, which the Army adopted as a standard service cartridge in 1963, in time for the Vietnam War.

Americans have always embraced American military service cartridges, so Remington wisely introduced the new cartridge as the .223 Remington shortly before the Army adopted it as the 5.56 x 45. It became a standard NATO cartridge in 1977.

The AR-15 was adopted in two variants as the M-16 (for the Air Force) and the XM-16E1 (for the Army), both of which were chambered for the new cartridge.

In 1965, the first large deployment of American troops entered combat in Vietnam, and the XM-16E1 was deployed with them.

The rigors of combat soon laid bare a number of problems with the new rifle, the details of which have been discussed thoroughly elsewhere. These problems were typical of a new technology in its infancy, unlike the mature, proven technology of the AK-47.

AK-47 versus AR-15/M-16: Apples versus Oranges

It is hard to imagine how two firearms could be more different and still be rivals in the shooting world. The AK-47 and its variants are utilitarian, idiot-proof military rifles that are cheap to produce and are ideal for issue to poorly-trained and uneducated conscript soldiers.

▲ Two old adversaries are seen here in civilian form, the .223 Remington 53-grain Match ammo (left) and the 7.62x39mm 124-grain hollow point (right). Known in military circles as the 5.56x45mm NATO, this cartridge provided the M-16's sting in Vietnam and other conflicts. Despite unfounded rumors to the contrary, the .223 Rem and the 5.56 NATO are perfectly interchangeable without any pressure issues. The 7.62x39 was a formidable foe in the AK-47 on battlefields around the world. In this hollowpoint load, it makes a pretty decent deer cartridge.

These weapons can withstand mud, sand, rust, extreme heat and cold, as well as neglect of even rudimentary maintenance, then still fire reliably when called upon. The receiver cover of one AK-47 confiscated from a poacher's camp in Zimbabwe was completely rusted away, exposing badly rusted operating parts within, and it still fired when the trigger was pulled.

If the AK-47 and its variants have a limitation it is that they are hopelessly one dimensional. If your objective is to equip a band of guerrillas or an army of poorly trained conscripts, the AK-47 is the runaway best choice. Also, it is probably the best choice for someone who is preparing to survive a major disaster by stockpiling weapons, food, and other essential supplies. But that's about it.

The AK-47 does not adapt well to any other use. It is not accurate enough for most sporting purposes, and you have only two choices of cartridges, the 7.62x39mm and the 5.45x39mm. Mounts for advanced weapon sights, such as the Trijicon ACOG, EOTech Holosight, any night vision scope, or even a conventional riflescope are fragile, cumbersome, and generally unsatisfactory.

A Great American Pastime

It is a time-honored tradition among young American males to tinker, tweak, chop, channel, and otherwise customize whatever toy is the object of their immediate interest. In the 1950s, it was hotrods, dragsters, and candy-apple red, pinstriped, souped-up street machines. As these tinkerers grew a bit older, they tinkered and tweaked custom audio equipment to emit sound so pure only an oscilloscope could appreciate it.

When personal computers came along in the eighties, they peered at the electronics inside and said to themselves, "I can build a better one than this." A few, including a tinkerer named Jobs, and a software geek named Gates, actually did.

A few others who were interested in shooting looked at the US Army service rifle and told themselves "This rifle could be really neat if I just changed one or two little things."

The rifle, of course, was the M-16 and its civilian counterpart, the AR-15. The AK-47 (along with its variations) is probably unsurpassed as an infantry weapon of warfare, but it is a one-trick pony. The AR-15, on

▲ Hadyn McDade fires his new custom AK-47 (see puffs of dirt downrange) with folding stock, quad rail, and vertical foregrip with tactical light.

the other hand, is something quite different. It is an American tinkerer's delight.

As the 1980s progressed into the 1990s, the AR-15 blossomed into a tack-driving competitive target rifle. It was modified to exchange the distinctive carry handle for a low profile picatinney rail for easy scope mounting. It sprouted a heavy bull barrel to reach out and touch prairie dogs—and a myriad of other variations along with accessories of every kind. New cartridge chamberings appeared from .204 Ruger for varmint hunting, to the .300 Whisper for use with a silencer, to the .50 Beowulf designed to drop America's heaviest game animals.

A Revolutionary Design Feature

The key to the AR-15's popularity among tinkerers/tweakers lies a little-discussed, but revolutionary design feature of the AR-15—modular construction.

The AR-15 has three easily interchangeable components (or modules). The first module is the lower receiver, which is serial numbered. This is the sole component of the AR-15 that is regulated as a firearm.

The lower receiver contains a semi-automatic trigger assembly, safety, magazine well, and pistol grip. The military M-16 differs chiefly because it has a full-auto trigger assembly that cannot readily be adapted to replace the semi-auto trigger in the civilian AR-15.

The lower receiver is the core of the AR-15. Everything else is merely an appendage. It's those appendages, however, that let the AR-15 blossom into the dazzling variety of calibers and configurations. Complete, separate lower receivers are available, which allow you to choose any available upper receiver or buttstock assembly to complete your AR-15.

For those who wish to take this process a step farther, stripped upper and lower receivers are available with parts kits and specialized tools. Assembling all the component parts of a lower (or upper) receiver is a satisfying and absorbing afternoon's project. It can also save you a few bucks compared to the cost of a complete rifle.

I have personally assembled five lower receivers, but have not yet tackled an upper receiver. I am only somewhat proficient with common hand tools and am definitely not a qualified gunsmith. However,

▲ Manufactured with a polymer upper and lower receiver, the Smith &Wesson M&P 15-22 is a lightweight .22 lr rifle that retains the controls and other features of the AR-15/M-16 platform. A picatinny quad rail comes standard on the M&P 15-22. The author's M&P 15-22 is "tricked-out" with a Bushnell Holosight by EOTech and a Surefire vertical foregrip with tactical light. It is an early production model without a flash hider, which is now standard on most M&P 15-22s.

I found the task to be well within my capabilities, and I definitely understand the inner workings of an AR-15 much better than I did before.

A Couple of Caveats

You should definitely invest in a book with step-by-step assembly instructions. Equally important are a few inexpensive, but essential assembly tools. These will be described in the instructions (see Appendix 2). Without these tools, the task will be daunting and frustrating. Instruction books, tools, and parts kits are readily available from such sources as Brownell's or Midway USA.

Contributing to the AR-15's versatility is the fact that neither the upper receiver nor the buttstock assembly are serial numbered, and both may be bought and sold without going through a Federal Firearms License holder.

Also contributing to this versatility, both the buttstock assembly and the upper receiver attach easily to the lower receiver without the services of a trained gunsmith.

Dozens of Options

By the 1980s, custom parts and components had become available for all three modules, which gave shooters dozens of options to customize or "trick out" their AR-15s.

The buttstock assembly is constructed around a buffer tube that contains the buffer and a large buffer spring. The buffer tube is threaded at the forward end to screw into a large attachment ring at the rear of the lower receiver. Until the early 1990s, civilian AR-15s were equipped with a fixed buttstock similar to the one on the military M-16A2. Then, the M4 carbine went into service with the US Army. This new weapon had a shorter barrel and a six-position, collapsible buttstock along with other features that made the M4 a more compact and versatile weapon than the M-16 A2.

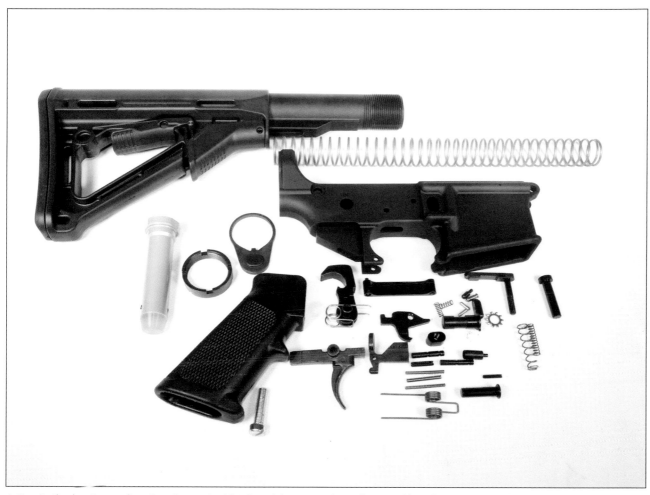

▲ Despite the daunting number of small parts, the AR-15's modular construction makes assembling a lower receiver and buttstock easy and enjoyable as a do-it-yourself project. Add an upper receiver and barrel assembly, and you are ready to head to the range. One point to remember—the stripped lower receiver shown above is considered to be a firearm by the BATFE. This means you must transfer it through a Federal Firearms License holder and complete a Form 4473 before you take possession. On the other hand, the upper receiver and barrel assembly are not a firearm and are legal to buy and sell without going through an FFL holder.

The new M4-style stock worked equally well on the civilian AR-15, and it did not take long for tricked-out versions of the collapsible buttstock to hit the civilian marketplace with built-up cheek pieces, spare magazine holders, or other unique features.

The upper receiver assembly attaches to the lower receiver by means of two pivot pins, one at the front of the lower receiver and another at the rear. The bolt and bolt carrier assembly are housed in the upper receiver.

At the forward end of the upper receiver is the barrel, which vents high-pressure combustion gas into the gas block/front sight pedestal. This fixture directs the combustion gas through a gas tube, into an expansion chamber on top of the bolt carrier. The barrel and gas tube are enclosed within either a two piece forend held in place by a hand guard retainer ring ("delta" ring) or a free-floating hand guard.

A "quad rail" forend may be substituted for the conventional two-piece forend. The quad rail has an additional picatinny rail at the top, bottom and each side of the forend. This provides sturdy mounting sites for accessories such as a vertical foregrip, tactical light, or other specialty items.

The barrel can be a lightweight 16-inch M4 type or a heavy "bull" barrel as long as 26 inches. It can be chambered in any of more than a dozen cartridges and equipped with a flash hider, threaded for a suppressor adapter or simply left with a bare muzzle.

As an alternative, the upper receiver assembly may substitute a gas piston operating system in place of the Stoner operating system. Also, at least one manufacturer offers a bolt-action conversion chambered for the powerful .50 BMG cartridge.

Personal Choices

In my personal AR-15 collection, you'll find a fixed-stock A2 National Match rifle for service rifle competition, a retired bull-barrel competition rifle for

▲ At a political fundraiser near Tucson, Arizona, Tyler Hartung tries out a collapsible-stocked AR-15 with Trijicon ACOG sight, quad rail, and vertical foregrip.

prairie dog shooting (the previous owner had replaced it when its accuracy degraded from .25 MOA to a tad under .5 MOA—ah well . . .), a .22 rimfire for plinking, a couple of tack-driving, silenced .300 Whispers, two M4s, and a 10-shot .177 caliber Benjamin pellet rifle. A couple have Harris bipods attached to their quad rail forends and there are a few vertical hand grips in the mix—one of which has a laser and very bright tactical strobe light.

In addition, I have another stripped lower receiver, collapsible buttstock assembly and an unused parts kit. I'm still trying to decide what niche that one will fill, but being one of those tinkerers mentioned earlier, I'll think of something.

▲ One of the more unusual AR conversions is this .177 caliber pellet upper from Benjamin, shown here attached to a Benjamin high pressure refill bottle. A removable 10-round magazine fits under the carry handle.

VI. Suppressed & Night Vision Firearms

We own the night!

"We own the night!" has been the mantra of America's ground forces in recent decades. But this was not always so. During the early days of the Vietnam War, the Viet Cong operated with near impunity during the hours of darkness. Then in 1965, the US Army equipped its troops with a secret weapon—a passive night vision device or NVD. NVDs came in three models: two were for battlefield surveillance and the third was the AV/PVS-2 weapon sight, popularly known as the starlight scope.

For the first time, American soldiers had a decisive advantage in night combat. The starlight scope played a major role in America's war effort in South Vietnam even though its weight and bulk made it unwieldy by today's standards. On numerous occasions, a starlight scope revealed enemy troops maneuvering to attack at night in time to call in artillery or air strikes that destroyed the attacking force.

Amazing Sniper Ambush

It was the night of February 14, 1969, at an artillery firebase near the Cambodian border. Marine sniper Sergeant Charles Benjamin (Chuck) Mawhinney and his spotter slipped out through the perimeter barbed wire and made their way to an ambush site overlooking a shallow crossing point on a nearby river, the Song Thu Bon.

Tonight, he was not carrying his beloved M40 (Remington Model 700 topped with a Redfield 3-9x variable power scope). Tonight, he carried an M14 battle rifle equipped with an AN/PVS-2 Starlight Scope. The M14 is a gas-operated semi-automatic rifle chambered for 7.62x51mm NATO, which is identical to the civilian .308 Winchester. It has a detachable box magazine that holds twenty rounds.

The two Marines settled into their positions in tall grass about 30 feet from the river and began their watch. The river was about 100 yards wide at this

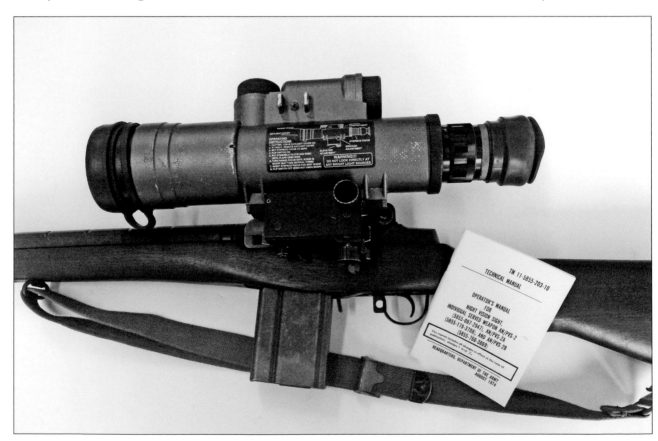

▲ Introduction of night vision weapon sights such as this AV/PVS-2 mounted on an M14, combined with similar battlefield surveillance devices gave the American military an enormous edge during the latter stages of the Vietnam War.

▲ Garry James's M14 is equipped with an AV/PS-2 starlight scope, similar to the rig used by Marine sniper Sergeant Chuck Mawhinney in Vietnam to kill 16 NVA soldiers within the space of thirty seconds as they attempted to cross a river.

point and no more than neck deep, shallow enough to wade.

About two hours after dark, a lone scout carrying a rifle emerged from the underbrush, eyes searching for signs of danger. He waded across the river and walked about. The scout came so close, Mawhinney recalled, that he could hear water dripping off his body.

As Mawhinney's finger tightened on the trigger, the scout turned suddenly, recrossed the river, and disappeared into the brush. Mawhinney held his fire and waited. He knew something was about to happen. About forty-five minutes to an hour later, a platoon of NVA soldiers appeared across the river and waded into the water in a staggered column about ten feet apart.

Watching through his starlight scope, Mawhinney waited until the point man emerged into knee-deep water at the river bank. With the reticle on the NVA's forehead, Mawhinney pressed his trigger and the soldier went down. Recovering from the M14's recoil, Mawhinney found the next target and fired again. After that, it was fire, acquire the next target, fire again. Within the space of thirty seconds, Mawhinney fired

sixteen times. Each time, an NVA soldier died instantly and floated down the river—all head shots.

As the remaining enemy force began to return fire from across the river, Mawhinney and his spotter low-crawled away from their firing position and exfiltrated back to the American firebase.

Not the first NVD

Although the starlight scope was the first useful *passive* night vision device, it wasn't the first attempt to see in the hours of darkness without being seen. *Active* night vision devices using infrared light date back before World War II.

The earliest NVDs used an infrared illuminator paired with an image converter. Radio Corporation of America (RCA) offered the first commercial NVD in the mid-1930s. The first military NVDs were developed by the German army as early as 1939. By 1943, some German Panther tanks were equipped with an NVD that used a powerful infrared searchlight to illuminate the battlefield.

The Wehrmacht fielded a few man-portable infrared weapon sights for the Sturmgewehr 44 assault rifle.

This device, the ZG 1229 Vampir, also employed an infrared searchlight.

The US Army also developed an infrared weapon sight during WWII designated as the M-1. This unit was very fragile and had an effective range of about 70 yards. By the Korean War, this had evolved to become the M3 Sniperscope. The M3 was mounted on a modified M2 carbine and had an effective range of about 125 yards.

The M3 was still very fragile. The scope could be damaged by exposure to direct sunlight. Also, the M3 employed a flash hider designed to shield the scope from muzzle flash as well as protect the shooter's night vision. This was only partially effective. Only about 2,100 modified M2 carbines were produced for the M3 Sniperscope, and it saw only limited actual battlefield use.

Fast forward to the Vietnam War, and night vision technology had advanced enormously with the introduction of the AN/PVS-2 Starlight Scope. Unlike the earlier M3, this was a "passive" night vision device, meaning that it did not use an illuminator of any sort, relying instead on amplifying available moon and star light to produce a visible image in the scope. It was used as a weapon sight for M14 and M-16 rifles and for battlefield surveillance.

Without an illuminator to give away the shooter's position, the AN/PVS-2 Starlight Scope gave a sniper a tremendous advantage as Chuck Mawhinney's exploit demonstrated in 1969.

The Vietnam era AN/PVS-2 Starlight Scope was a first generation (Generation I) passive night vision weapon sight, but it had a number of significant deficiencies. It was bulky and had poor resolution, which made target identification difficult. If it was suddenly exposed to a bright light source the scope would "bloom," blotting out the image entirely. In fact, a prolonged exposure to bright light could damage the intensifier tube beyond repair. Added to this was the fact that on overcast nights without sufficient moonlight, the AN/PVS-2 was near useless. Obviously, there was room for improvement.

Improvements Come Rapidly

Fueled by the ongoing Cold War, night vision technology advanced at a rapid pace. This is where writers are supposed to dazzle you with terminology such as *gallium-arsenide photo cathode*, *micro-channel plate*, *electrostatic conversion*, *ion barrier film*, *fiber optic inversion*, and the like. The truth is that night vision technology is wrapped up in peculiar electronic principles merged with certain optical properties and engineered into ever more sensitive, compact, and rugged weapon sights.

The details are of interest only to those who are willing to submerge themselves in arcane laws of physics. In plain language, light (photons) entering the objective lens of a night-vision device, strikes a charged plate. This causes the plate to emit electrons in a process that creates an image in a frequency the human eye can see.

Following the Generation I starlight scope of the Vietnam era, came Gen II devices with a much brighter image and significantly improved resolution. For the first time, civilian purchasers could own a night-vision weapon sight, although they cost significantly more than a top-of-the-line riflescope. Also, the US government

▲ The ARES 2-3 is a night-vision weapon sight that has a "red on green" reticle system with 1-6 MOA adjustment and 2x magnification. It has a one-knob operation, allows for precision windage and elevation adjustments, and mounts to standard weaver rails.
Credit: American Technologies Network Corporation

enacted regulations that prohibited export of NVDs under penalty of heavy fines and/or imprisonment.

Size and weight reductions resulted in night-vision goggles as well as helmet-mounted devices. Continued improvements became known as Gen II+, and night vision became available for helicopter pilots and vehicle drivers.

As the Soviet Union fell, Soviet military surplus night vision devices became available for only a few hundred dollars. Meanwhile, Gen III devices hit the civilian marketplace, and major corporations such as ITT, Litton, Raytheon, and others began marketing NVDs to the general public.

A New Type of Night Vision

From the earliest active infrared weapon sights to the latest passive image intensifiers, night-vision devices share one serious limitation. They all need at least a small amount of light to produce an image.

For an active infrared sight, this usually means an infrared spotlight mounted on the rifle to illuminate the target. A passive night-vision sight does not use an artificial light source (hence the term *passive*). Instead these devices rely on intensifying faint ambient illumination from moonlight or starlight to provide a visible image of the target.

However, there is an alternative—*thermal* night vision. A thermal sight employs a sensor that detects heat or thermal radiation, and the amount of radiation goes up with an object's temperature.

Trees, shrubbery, rocks, buildings, and other inanimate objects all radiate heat in varying amounts. A thermal imager can detect these small temperature differences and represent them as an image on a screen.

Warm-blooded animals, including humans, generate heat constantly and are almost always warmer than their surroundings. This allows a thermal imager to find animals despite natural camouflage or concealing vegetation—even in total darkness.

Unlike other types of night vision, thermal imaging works equally well in daylight and can even see through heavy fog or smoke. This is enormously important in military operations and can be very useful for night hunting where it's legal—usually for predators or feral hogs.

Thermal imaging also carries an enormous price tag with top-of-the-line weapon sights sometimes priced at more than $20,000. At the other end, basic units start in the neighborhood of $4,000. However, a thermal

▼ The ThOR-336 1.5X-6X (30Hz) is a thermal weapon sight that has a light and compact design, multiple color modes, and digital brightness control. It's also waterproof and can magnify up to 1.5 times.
Credit: American Technologies Network Corporation

weapon sight matched with the appropriate firearm offers unmatched performance—if you can afford it.

A Compatible Shooting Platform

American shooters have always been interested in military small arms including the M-16, which was first issued to American soldiers during the Vietnam War. Known as the black rifle, the M-16 was unlike any previous American service rifle, its aluminum receiver along with its plastic stock and forend was regarded as inferior to the honest steel and walnut of its predecessors. That eventually changed, and the black rifle began to earn respect.

By the early 1980s, its civilian counterpart, the semi-auto AR-15, had earned a reputation as an accurate choice for National Match service rifle competition. Because of its modular design, it was extremely versatile, and variations began to appear in a variety of (mostly wildcat) chamberings with collapsible stocks; short, lightweight barrels; long, heavy barrels; etc.

Perhaps the most interesting variation was the flat-top version, which exchanged the AR-15 carry handle for a picatinny rail to facilitate mounting a riflescope to take advantage of the AR-15's potential as a long range varmint rifle. This version also proved to be ideal for an NVD weapon sight.

When the federal assault weapons ban expired in 2004, a cottage industry sprang up to service a pent-up demand for black rifles and a wide assortment of after-market add-ons and accessories. Despite initial resistance, the growing community of black rifle shooters soon established the AR-15 as a legitimate hunting rifle, especially for varmints ranging from prairie dogs to coyotes.

No More Black Rifle

Today, it is no longer considered acceptable to refer to the AR-15 as a black rifle. Current wisdom says that sounds too menacing to non-shooters who might sway the balance in the voting booth. Now, we are told, we must call the AR-15 a Modern Sporting Rifle. Whatever we call the AR-15, equipping it with an infrared, image intensifying or thermal weapon sight makes a good combination for varmint calling at night or for ambushing feral hogs.

A Growing Menace

Let's take a moment to talk about the exploding population of feral hogs in rural America. Feral hogs are not a native species, and they have no natural predator species to keep their numbers in check—except man. In addition, they reproduce at an astonishing rate. A single sow can produce two litters of up to eight piglets each year.

Not surprisingly, feral hogs are expanding their range from the southeast United States into the Midwest and even farther, wreaking havoc on crops and pastureland as they go. The result is devastating agricultural losses costing tens of millions of dollars annually.

Hunting feral hogs is one of the best ways of controlling this growing menace, but hunting them successfully is a challenge. Because feral hogs are very intelligent, they react quickly to hunting pressure by becoming nocturnal. Even then, they remain wary, and the sound of gunfire will send them scurrying to cover.

This makes a night-vision-equipped firearm very useful for hunting feral hogs, especially a semi-automatic rifle that can engage several hogs rapidly before they can get outta Dodge.

One Final Piece of the Puzzle

As mentioned before, when a feral hog hears gunfire, it knows it's time to depart for less noisy places. Therefore, the well-equipped nighttime hog hunter needs to add one additional piece of the puzzle to complete his NVD-equipped rifle. That item is a silencer.

The silencer to muffle the report of a firearm was invented by Hiram Percy Maxim, the son of Hiram Stevens Maxim, who invented the first practical recoil-operated, portable machine gun. Nowadays, most people who think of themselves as experts will tell you that the term *silencer* is a misnomer. The idea is that the device does not completely obliterate the muzzle report of a firearm. It merely reduces the noise, they say, so the "correct" term is *suppressor*.

First of all, it ain't necessarily so.

I will concede that a bullet with a muzzle velocity greater than the speed of sound will produce a sharp *crack* that no silencer can reduce. This is actually a miniature sonic boom. However, if you use a *subsonic* cartridge, the bullet itself will generate virtually no noise as it emerges from the muzzle.

This author has witnessed a silencer-equipped sub-machine gun that was so nearly silent that the only perceivable noise was the sound of the bolt slapping shut at around 600 cycles per minute. Well, that's not entirely true. I could hear the rattling sound of .45 caliber bullets impacting the cardboard target 25 yards downrange. Other silencers might not be so effective, but that only means they were not as well-designed as this one.

Second, the inventor, Hiram Percy Maxim, called it a silencer. Who are we to dispute his terminology?

Third, if you should decide you want to own one, you will need to submit a properly completed ATF Form 4 to the federal government (along with the $200 transfer tax). Item 4b on that form identifies the device as a silencer. 'Nuff said.

While we're at it, there's a couple silencer myths that need refuting.

According to some "experts," a silencer reduces the velocity of a bullet as it passes through. Now that's a real head scratcher. The internal design of various silencers can differ considerably; however, none of them place obstructions in the bullet's path that could cause the bullet to lose velocity.

A silencer accomplishes its purpose by dissipating the high pressure gas produced when a cartridge is fired. It has no significant effect on the bullet—only the gases behind the bullet. Consider this myth busted.

We can't leave the topic of silencer myths without mentioning the infamous silencer-on-a-revolver myth. Clueless Hollywood scriptwriters and gun-ignorant novelists can't seem to get it through their heads that you *cannot* silence a revolver—at least not with a device such as what we are discussing here.

The culprit is the flash gap. The flash gap is a space several thousandths of an inch wide between the forward face of the revolver cylinder and the rear face of the barrel. When the revolver is fired, high pressure gases erupt from this gap with enough force to cause serious injury if you are careless enough to allow a finger (or other body part) to stray too close.

It is also very loud.

Besides revolvers, some other firearms are not compatible with a silencer, particularly blow-back operated firearms. Most blow-back actions begin to extract while chamber pressure is still very high. This allows some high pressure gas to escape from the breech, which as you might guess is very noisy, rendering a silencer ineffective.

So, one last, persistent myth is busted. Now, if only we could get Hollywood to listen.

Supersonic versus Subsonic Ammo

Several factors determine how effectively a silencer will reduce or eliminate muzzle blast. First, the volume of high velocity gas propelling the bullet: this gas must be slowed and dissipated before it escapes at the muzzle.

Second, the design of the silencer: inside most silencers is an expansion chamber and a series of baffles designed to reduce pressure and disrupt pressure wave fronts. The greater the volume of gas, the more internal volume the silencer must have to accomplish this. Accordingly, a small silencer designed for the .22 long rifle cartridge would be totally inadequate for a high energy centerfire cartridge such as the .223 Remington.

Third, bullet velocity: a bullet with a muzzle velocity higher than the speed of sound will create a shock wave—actually a sonic boom. This produces a loud *crack* that travels downrange with the bullet. To prevent this, the bullet must leave the muzzle *below* the speed of sound. This can be done by reducing the powder charge (which also reduces the amount of high velocity gas to be dissipated) or increasing the bullet's weight—or both.

Many pistol cartridges, such as the .45 ACP, are subsonic in normal full-power loads. So, no modification for use with a silencer would be necessary. However, pistol cartridges are designed for use at short range. What about high-velocity rifle cartridges suitable for use at longer ranges?

Unlike pistol bullets, rifle bullets are typically more aerodynamic with pointed noses and in some cases boat-tailed rear sections. This would reduce bullet drag in flight, resulting in higher retained downrange velocity.

Although many different rifle bore diameters are suitable for pairing with a silencer, the .30 caliber is one of the most versatile. This author has had some experience with silencers for this bore size, and I've made some remarkable discoveries. One of my most interesting discoveries is the .300 Whisper cartridge developed by J. D. Jones, a well-known cartridge designer from Ohio. J. D.'s company, SSK Industries, is well known for his custom firearms, ranging from his JDJ hand cannons based on Thompson/Center Contenders and Encores to specialized tactical equipment, including silencers and AR-15/M-16/M4 based tactical rifles.

An Ideal Cartridge

Working with special operations personnel from the US military, J. D. accepted the challenge of developing a suppressed weapon based on the M-16/M4 platform for spec ops missions. The unique requirements for such a weapon demanded development of a new cartridge.

The new cartridge would need to be subsonic for use with a silencer, but have enough power to put down a determined enemy. It should also be capable of effectively engaging enemy troops at several hundred meters. It had to do all of these things within the confines of the M-16/M4 platform, but with only minimal modifications.

J. D. designed the .300 Whisper late in 1992 and copyrighted the name of this remarkable cartridge in November of that year. He created the .300 Whisper by necking up the .221 Remington Fireball to .30

caliber with no other modifications. Similar .30-221 wildcat cartridges had been around for a long time, but the .300 Whisper was the first specifically designed as a subsonic round for a silencer-equipped M-16.

The .300 Whisper's head size and overall length is nearly identical to the 5.56 NATO/.223 Remington, so it will fit into and feed normally from an unmodified G. I. M-16 magazine. This means that no modifications are necessary to convert an M-16 to fire the .300 Whisper—other than replacing the 5.56 NATO barrel with a .30 caliber barrel chambered for .300 Whisper.

The Sporting Arms and Ammunition Manufacturers Institute (SAAMI) does not recognize the .300 Whisper because of an internal policy not to recognize cartridges with copyrighted names. *This does not make the .300 Whisper a wildcat.*

Actually, the .300 Whisper *is recognized as standard* by an international body, the *Commission Internationale Permanente pour l'Épreuve des Armes à Feu Portatives* (CIP). This influential body has fourteen member nations, including Austria, Belgium, Germany, France, Italy, Spain, Russia, and the United Kingdom.

In addition, two major ammunition manufacturers now offer .300 Whisper ammo both in supersonic and in subsonic loadings. Also, at least two major firearms manufacturers (other than SSK Industries) chamber firearms for the .300 Whisper. This definitely takes the .300 Whisper out of the wildcat class and places it firmly into standard status. (See Table 1 for .300 Whisper factory ballistic data.)

▼ Table 1. .300 Whisper Factory Ballistics

	Bullet Weight	Muzzle Velocity	Muzzle Energy
CorBon	125 gr	2,100 fps	1,224 ft lb
CorBon	150 gr	1,900 fps	1,203 ft lb
CorBon	220 gr	1,040 fps	529 ft lb
Hornady	110 VMax	2,375 fps	1,377 ft lb
Hornady	208 Amax	1,020 fps	480 ft lb

Handloading the .300 Whisper

Handloading data for the .300 Whisper is available from several sources. However, I must express a cautionary note: *Never, ever use any load data obtained on the Internet*—unless it is published from an established ammo or firearms manufacturer.

Having said that, SSK Industries (the originator of the .300 Whisper) has some of the most thoroughly tested data for the .300 Whisper, and it is available from SSK at a nominal cost. Time for another cautionary note: For subsonic loads, *do not "work up"* your load from a reduced starting load! If you do, you run the risk of leaving a bullet lodged firmly in the barrel.

Subsonic loads in the .300 Whisper—or any other subsonic centerfire cartridge—generate very low pressure, so reducing the powder charge too far can result in a bullet becoming stuck in the bore. This can be very dangerous, if the stuck bullet goes undetected and another round is fired. It can also ruin an expensive barrel.

Handloaders also need to be aware that a barrel with a fast 1-in-8-inch twist is necessary for .300 Whisper subsonic loads using bullets heavier than 210 grains. A 1-in-10-inch twist is okay for loads using 210-grain bullets or lighter.

What is my favorite subsonic handload for the .300 Whisper?

Answer: 9.8 grains of H110 with a Sierra 240-gr BTSP, which gives me about 1,070 fps in my Smith & Wesson M&P-15.

A Bold Marketing Strategy

In 2010, a "new" cartridge (please notice the quotation marks) was introduced. In a heavily financed marketing campaign, the .300 AAC Blackout was launched and touted as the perfect cartridge for use with a silencer on the AR-15/M4 platform. (The parent company insists on calling the device a suppressor. Call it what you want, you know my opinion.) The cartridge uses the standard AR-15 bolt assembly and the standard AR-15/M-16/M4 magazine with no other modifications except a .30 caliber barrel chambered for the new round—*just like the .300 Whisper does.*

The parent company will tell you that a military customer came to them in 2009 with a requirement for a cartridge with the above stated qualities for use in a suppressed M4 platform. The company started development and in 2010, a completely *original* design—the .300 Blackout—was born.

Oddly, the new cartridge's chamber dimensions are nearly identical to the .300 Whisper. Even odder, the .300 Whisper was designed for a US military customer eighteen years—nearly two decades—earlier, in 1992.

Adding even more oddities to the mix, that 1992 military customer wanted the .300 Whisper to use the M4's standard, unmodified bolt carrier group and the standard, unmodified G.I. M4/M-16 magazine—which it does, flawlessly.

The .300 Blackout's parent company was able to obtain a SAAMI standard listing for the .300 Blackout, and they use this fact to suggest that the .300 Whisper is somehow unsafe because of the existence of non-standard chamber reamers and loading dies with dimensions that vary considerably.

This, of course, is absurd.

Barrels and loading dies chambered for .300 Whisper and so marked have tolerances that are strictly enforced by SSK Industries. In addition, CorBon and Hornady use identical cartridge cases for the .300 Whisper and the .300 Blackout, changing only the headstamp. CorBon offers loaded ammunition for both cartridges. Hornady offers .300 Whisper ammunition, but cartridge cases only for the .300 Blackout.

Smith & Wesson also regards these two cartridges as identical. They barrel-stamp 300 Whisper/300 AAC Blackout on their M&P-15 rifles, marking them as suitable to shoot both cartridges.

The bottom line is that the .300 Whisper and the .300 AAC Blackout are identical for all practical purposes. They both work flawlessly through AR-15/M4 rifles chambered for either cartridge.

The .308 Winchester/7.62 x 51mm NATO

A growing number of tactical rifles chambered for .308 Winchester/7.62 x 51mm NATO are hitting the marketplace. This includes exotic, semi-custom rifles from companies such as McMillan Firearms to more traditional rifles from Remington, Ruger, Savage, and others.

It was adopted by the US military in 1954, but it didn't see actual service until 1957 when the government began issuing the M-14 service rifle and M-60 machine gun to active Army combat units. During the Vietnam War, when marine sergeant Chuck Mawhinney ambushed and killed sixteen enemy soldiers during a night river crossing, his M-14 rifle was chambered for the 7.62 x 51mm service cartridge.

During its service life, the 7.62 x 51mm has earned a reputation as a reliable cartridge capable of effective aimed fire at more than 1,000 meters. Because it has been an official NATO service cartridge since the mid-1950s, it has been manufactured by almost every one of the signatory nations and is widely available as imported surplus ammunition.

Internet-inspired Myths

A couple of unfounded myths concerning the 7.62 NATO vs the .308 Winchester have emerged since the advent of the internet. Myth number one contends that 7.62 NATO ammunition is loaded to higher pressure than .308 Winchester and is unsafe to fire in rifles chambered for .308 Winchester. Myth number two says the headspace is so much greater in 7.62 military rifles that the thinner brass of commercial .308 Winchester ammo will stretch and separate at the base, releasing high pressure gas and create general havoc.

Here are the facts, starting with myth number one:

The Copper Crusher Method

When the 7.62 NATO was adopted, the pressure criterion was Copper Units of Pressure (CUP). This method of pressure testing uses a pressure barrel, that has a hole drilled into the side of the chamber, which is fitted with a piston. The piston bears against a copper cylinder of precise dimensions. When the test cartridge is fired, the chamber pressure slams the piston against the cylinder, deforming (or crushing) it. The amount of deformation is proportional to the amount of chamber pressure exerted against it. The deformed cylinder is measured to determine how much it was deformed and the result is expressed as Copper Units of Pressure or (CUP). The acceptable pressure limit for the 7.62 NATO cartridge is 52,000 CUP.

This was often called 52,000 pounds per square inch (psi), but this was (and is) not correct. CUP and psi

simply are *not* the same thing. Making things worse, the Copper Crusher method is woefully inaccurate.

The amount of crushing can vary depending on how hard the copper cylinder is and the purity of the copper (which affects its density). To complicate matters even more, a new copper cylinder might give a different result than an old one that has been on hand for a few years because copper (and many other metals) gets slowly harder with age.

The Piezoelectric Method

Today, the industry standard method to test a cartridge's chamber pressure uses a piezoelectric crystal embedded in the chamber of a pressure barrel. When a cartridge is fired, the chamber pressure exerts mechanical stress on the crystal, generating a small electrical current.

This method yields an actual pressure/time curve that gives a much more complete picture of what happens when a cartridge is fired. With this method, the maximum peak pressure limit established for most cartridges is around 62,000 psi. Now here is the confusing part. Because the Copper Crusher method and the piezoelectric method are measuring two distinctively different things, they produce distinctively different numbers in most cases. In the case of the 7.62 NATO rated at 52,000 CUP and the .308 Winchester at 62,000 psi (piezoelectric method), *the chamber pressures are roughly the same.*

Unfortunately, some ignorant souls don't realize that and assume that .308 Winchester ammo is unsafe to fire in a 7.62 NATO chamber. What makes this assertion border on pathetic is the fact that modern rifles (military or commercial) must fire a *75,000 psi proof cartridge* without damage before they leave the factory.

Myth number two states that most military rifles—especially machine guns—have slightly greater headspace to ensure battlefield reliability with dirty or out-of-spec ammo (true). It also says that the walls and base (or web) of military 7.62 NATO brass is thicker than commercial .308 Winchester ammo (sometimes true; sometimes, not).

The myth states with a (smug) air of authority that if you fire a .308 Winchester cartridge in a military 7.62 chamber, the thinner .308 brass will stretch to fill the longer chamber, causing the cartridge to separate when it is fired. This will cause the gun to blow up, the myth says.

Here are the facts on myth number two:

Yes, if you fire a .308 case in a longer-than-standard chamber, the case wall will stretch. So will the thicker 7.62 NATO case wall, but possibly slightly less. This will also happen in a standard .308 chamber to a lesser degree, and the same is true of the 7.62 NATO. *In neither instance will a previously unfired cartridge stretch enough to separate.*

Caveat for Handloaders

Now, if you take that stretched case, whether it is a .308 or a 7.62 NATO, and full-length resize it with the loading die screwed down to touch the shellholder, prime it, add the powder charge, seat the bullet and fire it again—it will stretch more, and the case wall will get slightly thinner each time.

If you are stupid enough to repeat this process again and again, you will notice that the case neck seems to get slightly longer each time until you have to trim it back to the proper length. Somewhere between five or ten reloads, maybe more, you might experience a head separation and find hot combustion gases venting into your rifle's action.

If you resize a cartridge case as described above, you resize it to minimum dimensions. If you then fire it in a maximum dimension chamber, it will stretch to conform to the available space, which causes the case wall to become just slightly thinner.

Resizing it and firing it this way repeatedly will continue the process until the case becomes thin enough to cause a head separation. Most modern rifle actions are designed to vent the erupting high pressure gas away from the shooter's face, but you might still suffer injuries of some sort and possible damage to your rifle.

In a best case scenario, you have the front half of your cartridge case stuck in the chamber, which will probably require a competent gunsmith to remove it. Even if there is no other damage or injuries, this is still a major pain in the neck.

To prevent this, a savvy handloader will use a candle to smoke the neck of a fired round. Then, he would adjust the sizing die according to the instructions below:

Having unscrewed the sizing die lock ring, place the cartridge in the shellholder and raise the ram of the loading press all the way. Now screw the sizing die into the press and over the cartridge until it meets resistance.

After lowering the ram, screw the die about a quarter-inch farther down, then cycle the ram up and down. The cartridge neck should be shiny where the die sized the neck down. The base of the neck and the shoulder should still be smoke-blackened where the die did not reach.

Now, gradually lower the die a fraction at a time and repeat the process until the case neck is fully resized without setting back the shoulder. Now screw the locking ring all the way down and tighten the set screw.

This will neck-size the cartridge case instead of full-length resizing it. Your reloaded ammo might not seat fully in a tighter chamber, *but it will fit perfectly in the same rifle the case was fired in.*

Also, case stretching will be minimal, greatly reducing the likelihood of a case separation.

Back To The Program

Having dispensed with internet myths, let's get back to talking about the merits of the .308 Winchester/7.62 NATO in silencer equipped rifle.

Less Than Ideal

A normal 150-grain factory load for the .308 leaves the muzzle just north of 2,800 fps, which is nearly two and a half times the speed of sound. This produces a loud sonic boom. A silencer designed to handle the volume of gas produced by a .308 can deal with the muzzle blast, but it can do nothing to silence the loud crack that generates continuously as the bullet speeds downrange at a half-mile per second. Despite the lack of muzzle blast to mark where the shot came from, the above-mentioned loud crack still informs anyone within hearing distance that a gun has been fired.

That's the bad news. Here's the good news: as the traveling bullet continues to generate its sonic boom, it draws an observer's attention away from the location of the shooter. Also, echoes bounce off any hard object en route, which further confuses an observer's ear.

The bottom line is that despite the noise of a supersonic bullet, it's very difficult to determine where it came from. In a wartime ambush, this makes return fire less effective. In hunting varmints or a pack of feral hogs, the confusion can give the shooter an opportunity to score multiple kills before the animals can make good their escape.

Subsonic .308 Winchester Loads

Subsonic .308 Winchester ammo greatly increases the effectiveness of a silencer-equipped .308/7.62 tactical rifle. Currently, two ammo makers offer subsonic .308 Winchester ammo, CorBon and McMillan.

CorBon's Performance Match subsonic .308 Winchester load is tipped with a 185-grain full metal jacket, rebated boattail match-grade bullet that leaves the muzzle at 1070 fps with 411 ft lbs of energy. Assembled with specially selected match-grade com-

ponents, CorBon subsonic .308 delivers outstanding accuracy under all conditions.

McMillan's Tactical .308 Winchester subsonic loading is formulated for optimum performance in the McMillan Alias CS5 Concealable Subsonic/supersonic Suppressed Sniper System. Tipped with a 200-grain Match-grade bullet, McMillan tactical .308 subsonic ammo uses a powder charge selected for consistent velocity to minimize vertical spread at extreme long range.

The CS5 is a state-of-the-art, precision tactical rifle that breaks down into a package only 23.5 inches long and is designed to use an Elite Iron Bravo silencer.

The CS5 has a 12.5-inch, stainless steel barrel that is capable of .5 MOA or better with McMillan Tactical

▼ Several ammo manufacturers now offer sub-sonic ammo for use with an AR-15 chambered for .300 Whisper and equipped with a suppressor. Subsonic ammo also is available for suppressor-equipped tactical rifles chambered in .308 Winchester.

▲ Designed for stealth and concealment, the McMillan ALIAS CS5 is a compact precision tactical rifle. Configured with a suppressor, the CS5 can be purchased under NFA regulations by submitting an ATF Form 4 and paying the $200 transfer tax.

subsonic ammo or with supersonic match-grade ammo. Because of the short barrel, NFA regulations apply to its purchase.

Fair Chase Does Not Apply

The exploding population of feral hogs is becoming an agricultural disaster of epic proportions, so many states have relaxed their hunting regulations (at least concerning feral hogs) to give hunters some leverage in controlling hog populations. Nowhere is this more true than in Texas where night hunting for hogs with night vision- and suppressor-equipped firearms is perfectly legal. Even shooting hogs from a helicopter has the blessing of Texas authorities.

With a Texas hog-hunting expedition in my immediate future, I will probably pass up helicopter sniping, but I have assembled a few toys and accoutrements to facilitate the operation.

Hog Medicine Numero Uno

At the top of my list is an SSK Industries .300 Whisper AR-15 upper with an SSK screw-on silencer. This is mated to an Aero Precision lower receiver that I bought as a stripped lower receiver. I assembled it using a Brownell's lower receiver parts kit and assembly tools.

The SSK upper receiver has a 16-inch stainless steel barrel with a 1-in-7.5-inch twist to stabilize the heaviest bullets in subsonic loads. A unique feature is the SSK's adjustable gas block that ensures 100 percent reliability with supersonic as well as subsonic loads. A coin-slotted switch on top of the tubular forend has an "H"

▲ The T14X thermal night vision scope can double as a handheld night vision unit as well as a riflescope.

and an "L" setting. Turning the switch so the "L" faces the shooter, sets the gas block to feed subsonic ammo perfectly. Supersonic ammo will function properly on the "L" setting, but will place unnecessary stress on the action. In the "H" position, supersonic loads function perfectly, but subsonic loads will not cycle the action.

The SSK silencer is designed for .308 Winchester/7.62 NATO, so it easily handles the relatively small volume of combustion gas generated by the .300 Whisper. When the 12-inch device is properly installed, the muzzle end of the barrel extends a full six inches inside the voluminous expansion chamber, so only the silencer's remaining six inches extends beyond the muzzle.

Sighting equipment is a T14X digital thermal weapon sight (FLIR) made by Sierra Pacific Innovations (SPI). At 2.18 pounds, the T14X is about twice as heavy as most optical riflescopes, but its night imaging capability more than makes up for the difference. The unit has a 1–2x zoom capability, but the manufacturer does

not recommend shooting or sighting-in at the higher power setting. The T14X is only 7 inches long, and has a flexible rubber eye guard that adds 2 more inches. The T14X attaches to the flat-top SSK's picatinny rail by a throw lever, quick-detachable mount.

The shooter can choose from eight color and black-and-white image modes and can record video or still images to an SD card in the device's battery compartment. Because it uses thermal imaging the T14X does not rely on visible light and can operate in total darkness. For the same reason, the T14X works well in daylight, too. It's a simple matter of scrolling through the eight image modes to see which one works best in the current situation.

My SSK AR-15 in .300 Whisper equipped with its SSK silencer and SPI T14X thermal weapon sight is a very accurate combination, that hovers around 1 MOA with Hornady factory ammo or my favorite handloads.

▼ Equipped and ready for a night-time hog hunt, the S&W M&P15 (top) is chambered for .300 Whisper and fitted with a SureFire suppressor and ATN Gen II+ night vison scope. Also ready to go is an Aero Precision lower receiver (bottom) mated to an SSK Industries upper receiver assembly chambered for .300 Whisper with SSK suppressor. It is topped by a T14X thermal weapon sight by Sierra Pacific Innovations.

▲ Ruger's Gunsite Scout Rifle, chambered for .308 Winchester, needed a few modifications to set it up for a SureFire suppressor and night vision device. I replaced the Ruger flash hider with a SureFire adapter/flash hider and attached a UTG barrel mount triple rail to accommodate a pair of SureFire white/IR tactical lights. Then I replaced the forward mounted Ruger picatinny rail with an XS Ruger/GSR rail that extends back to attach to the rear receiver ring. Finally, I mounted an Elcan Digital Day/Night Hunter infrared night sight to make it fully capable for hog culling at night. With subsonic .308 ammo and the SureFire suppressor, it is quiet and deadly at night. With normal, full-power .308 ammo, the GSR is a capable tactical or hunting rifle—with or without a supressor.

Hog Medicine Numero Dos

Running a close second in my .300 Whisper lineup is my Smith & Wesson M&P-15 with Realtree™ APG camo finish. It is fitted with a flash hider/adapter for a SureFire FA762K silencer. The M&P's 16-inch barrel is 4140 steel with a 1 in 7.5-inch twist. It is marked 300 Whisper/300 AAC Blackout, attesting to the two cartridges' interchangeability. The fast twist gives the M&P (like the SSK) the ability to stabilize the heaviest bullets in .300 Whisper subsonic ammo.

On top of the M&P-15 is an ATN Night Arrow 4 Gen II night vision weapon sight with 4X magnification. At 3.1 pounds, this sight is a bit heavier than the T14X thermal scope mentioned above. Unlike the T14X, the Night Arrow 4 does rely on ambient light however faint to produce a useable image.

On the plus side, the Night Arrow 4 has good image resolution, and an excellent reticle with a variable intensity red center cross hair that can be adjusted to the shooter's preference. Also, its objective lens cap has a small filtered aperture that makes the Night Arrow 4 useable in daylight as well the hours of darkness.

The Night Arrow 4, paired with my SureFire silencer-equipped Smith & Wesson M&P-15, is a fine choice for night hunting feral hogs.

Along with my SSK/SureFire/T14X combo, these two rifles are a stealthy and potent pair for hunting feral hogs at night.

Hog Medicine Numero Tres

I wanted something with a longer range potential for my third silenced, night vision hog rifle, so I chose a left-hand, blued steel Ruger Gunsite Scout Rifle or GSR.

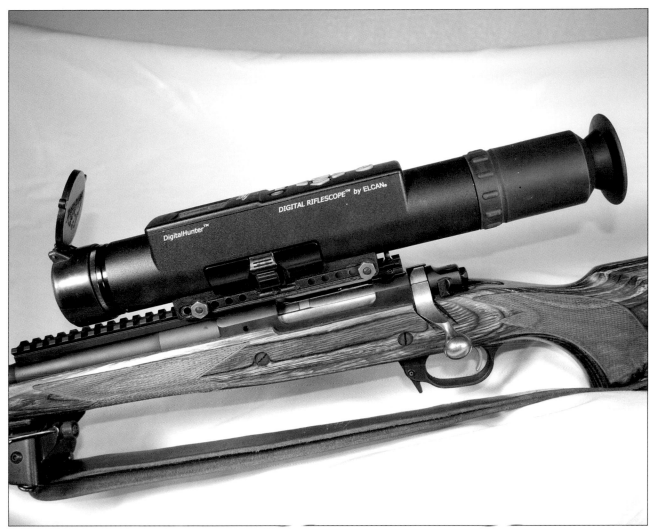

▲ Elcan's Digital Day/Night Hunter is not a riflescope, but an "optronic" 2.5-16X zoom sighting device with an infrared night vision capability. Essentially, it is a television camera with as many as four different aiming reticles available by simply pushing a button. It also has an internal ballistics program and can take still photos and short video sequences.

The GSR is a worthy example of the scout rifle concept advocated by Colonel Jeff Cooper for many years. Despite what some nitpickers might say, I believe that after looking it over carefully, the good Colonel would have nodded and given his approval.

Using the time-tested M77 action mated to a 16.5-inch barrel, the GSR is available in a left- or right-hand version with your choice of stainless steel or blued alloy steel. The black-laminated wood stock, forward-mounted picatinny rail, ghost ring rear sight, detachable box magazine and flash hider are standard.

Chambered for .308 Winchester, the GSR is a dual threat. Normal supersonic .308 ammo is effective beyond a half-mile. In wartime, American snipers have scored kills at 1,000 meters and more.

Before I could add the GSR to my battery of hog rifles, I needed to add a few accessories. First, I attached a Harris bipod to the forend sling swivel stud. This was a no-brainer since Colonel Cooper considered a folding bipod to be an essential part of his scout rifle concept.

Next, I replaced the barrel-mounted picatinny rail with a full-length rail from XS Sight Systems. This 11.5-inch rail uses the existing attachment screws and extends back to the rear receiver ring.

This permits mounting a riflescope with conventional eye relief on the GSR receiver. It also permits attachment of a Digital Day/Night Hunter weapon sight made by Raytheon's EO Innovations division. This unit has a passive infrared capability for use at night, but it needs a source of infrared illumination to work properly.

For infrared illumination, I chose a pair of lightweight SureFire M600V Scout Lights, which can switch between a high-output white light LED and a

▲ The Objective Lens cover of this Gen II night vision riflescope protects the internal components from damage caused by exposure to bright light conditions. However, the small aperture on the lens cover admits enough light to sight-in during daylight hours.

high-output infrared LED. A UTG tri-rail barrel mount clamps the two lights side by side onto the GSR's barrel about six inches aft of the muzzle. I chose not to use the M600V's pressure activated tape switches. Instead I use the simpler tailcap switch found on most SureFire tactical lights.

That took care of the night vision accessories, but I needed to make one last modification to attach a silencer to my GSR hog rifle. Unscrewing the flash hider on the GSR's muzzle, I replaced it with a SureFire flash hider, which doubles as an adapter for an FA762K silencer.

Despite the add-ons and accoutrements, my Ruger GSR is a well-balanced, manageable package. Using subsonic .308 ammo from CorBon and McMillan, my Numero Tres hog medicine is stealthy and mission-ready for a nighttime feral hog ambush.

Barring unforeseen events, my night vision and silencer-equipped hog-hunting battery will make its debut in the early fall, just before Texas deer season.

VII. Ultra-Big-Bore Sniper Rifles

A discussion of ultra-big-bore sniper rifles must begin with the man who defined the subject of long-range sniping for the modern era: Gunnery Sergeant Carlos N. Hathcock II, USMC.

In 1967, Hathcock killed a Viet Cong guerrilla at a range of 2,500 yards (2,286 meters). I included the metric equivalent because the US military has used the metric system since 1957 to conform to NATO standards of distance measurement. Therefore, Hathcock's record kill shot would have been recorded in metric units of measure, or 2,286 meters.

Hathcock used a Browning M2 .50 caliber machine gun to make his shot. He improvised a scope mount to attach a 10-power Unertl riflescope to the "Ma Deuce" and set out to stalk his victim. Using a Browning M2 as a sniper weapon did not originate with Hathcock. Other such incidents date back to the Korean War, but Hathcock's record shot is the only one authenticated and confirmed.

It is necessary to understand a few additional things about Hathcock's record shot. First, there were no laser rangefinders to reach out a mile and a half to measure distances within a few inches. However, artillery surveying equipment and accurate topographic maps were available to obtain an accurate distance. Also, the Marine Corps required a commissioned officer to confirm a sniper kill before it could be recorded as such. So there can be no doubt, Hathcock's record kill is authentic.

The Mighty .50 BMG

The story of ultra-big-bore sniper rifles is inextricably linked to the awesome .50 caliber Browning Machine Gun cartridge (.50 BMG), also known as the 12.7x99mm NATO. The .50 BMG was developed near the end of World War I as a heavy machine gun cartridge for anti-aircraft use and is simply a scaled-up .30-06 cartridge. Along with the M2 Browning machine gun it was designed for, the .50 BMG is one of the most successful military weapon combinations of all time. It has even been immortalized in the lexicon of American slang in the expression "the whole nine yards," which refers to the 27-foot length of linked .50 BMG ammo that WWII American fighter planes carried for each on-board .50 caliber machine gun.

Officially adopted in 1921, the .50 BMG still serves the US military in a variety of roles, including long-range sniping.

A misconception exists in some quarters that international treaty bans the use of the .50 BMG against human targets; however, the US government position is that no such ban exists on the .50 BMG.

Under federal regulation, a .50 caliber firearm is the largest caliber that can be civilian-owned and transferred without designation as a "destructive device" under the 1934 National Firearms Act. Although the bullet diameter of the .50 BMG is .510 inches, the bore diameter measured across the rifling lands of a rifle chambered for .50 BMG is a legal .50 inches. However, some states (notably California) restrict or outlaw ownership of such firearms.

Barrett M82A1

Oddly, nearly seventy years went by before the military acquired a .50 BMG firearm designed as a sniper weapon, the Barrett M82A1.

Founded by Ronnie Barrett, Barrett Firearms Manufacturing was launched in the early 1980s to market his semi-automatic rifle designed for the .50 BMG cartridge. Production of the new rifle began in 1982, and accordingly, it was designated the M82.

Featuring a rotating bolt, recoil-operated action, the M82 had a 10-round box magazine; an adjustable, folding bipod; and a picatinny rail for mounting a riflescope. By 1986, an improved version, the M82A1 had been developed, and Barrett landed its first military contract in 1989, selling about 100 M82A1s to the Swedish Army. The US Marine Corps initially bought small numbers of the semi-automatic Barrett M82A1 in .50 BMG during Desert Shield in 1990. Orders from the US Army and Air Force soon followed.

The American military intended the M82A1 to be used as an anti-materiél weapon to destroy lightly armored vehicles, bunkers and similar fortifications. It was also to be used in an Explosive Ordnance Disposal (EOD) role. Its use as a long-range, anti-personnel weapon relegated to a secondary role.

As the 1990s progressed, the Barrett M82A1 saw service with the military and police of nearly three dozen countries, including Great Britain, Belgium, France, and Germany. By the turn of the century, the Barrett

▲ A 10-round detachable magazine on an accurate semi-auto .50 BMG rifle such as the Barrett M82A1 gives a military sniper awesome firepower for missions at extreme long range.

brand had established itself as the Gold Standard for large-bore military small arms, a reputation that stands to this day.

The Barrett M82A1 comes disassembled in a sturdy Pelican-type case. It can be assembled by following the enclosed instructions carefully. However, I found it a bit tricky to get the pieces together properly. To assemble the upper receiver, you must insert the barrel key into its proper recess against the tension of the twin barrel springs.

According to the instruction manual, spring tension is 70 pounds, and it is every bit of that, if not more. Pulling against this tension is difficult, made especially so because there is very little to grasp and pull against. The instructions also tell you not to grasp the two springs, which are vulnerable to damage. With much effort, we finally got the barrel key inserted

properly and were ready to attach the upper to the lower receiver.

To do this, you must remove two retaining pins before mating the upper and lower. Then you must insert the front hook on the upper to its seat in the lower receiver before completing assembly. Here is where a caution banner in the instructions tells you it is easy to bend the front hook at this point, which will cause serious damage to the rifle and render it incapable of being fired.

I find this fragility unacceptable in a combat weapon. It is definitely not soldier proof.

Having said that, I still enjoyed shooting the M82A1. However, the recoil was noticeably more pronounced with the Barrett than with my Armalite AR-50L bolt-action .50. I recorded no malfunctions of any kind with the Barrett while putting just under 100

▲ A single armor-piercing incendiary round from this .50 BMG Barrett Model 82A1 found something flammable in this derelict target auto. A few moments later, a small flame licked up out of the engine compartment and eventually engulfed the car.

▲ The Barrett M82A1 .50 BMG semi-auto sniper rifle, shown here being fired by Tyler Hartung, was the first semi-auto .50 caliber rifle available. After three decades of development, the M82A1 is still one of the best choices for extreme long-range sniper missions.

rounds downrange. Accuracy was acceptable, but not spectacular.

McMillan TAC-50

Spectacular accuracy, however, is a beautiful thing, and it is absolutely essential when the range to your target approaches a mile and a half. As with smaller caliber rifles, the easiest and most certain way to get spectacular accuracy in a rifle chambered for .50 BMG is to insist on a bolt-action. This brings us to one of the best of the ultra-big-bore bolt action rifles, the McMillan TAC 50.

In 1973, Gale McMillan pioneered fiberglass synthetic stocks, making them on his kitchen table. That same year, Millard McMillan set a world record for accuracy in sanctioned bench rest competition that stands to this day. McMillan's 100-yard, 5-shot group was fired with a hand-built prototype McMillan rifle bedded to one of the first McMillan fiberglass stocks. The

group measured 0.009 inches (center-to-center). The cartridge was the .222 Remington.

As the fledgling company grew and expanded its product line into complete rifles, the McMillan name began to represent the pinnacle of rifle accuracy.

In 1996, McMillan designed the TAC-50 rifle chambered for .50 BMG and immediately raised the accuracy bar for ultra-big-bore rifles. The TAC-50 is a bolt-action rifle with a 29-inch, fluted barrel; synthetic stock with an adjustable cheek piece; efficient muzzle brake; and a folding bipod. It feeds from a detachable five-round magazine.

In 2001, McMillan secured a contract to supply TAC-50 rifles to the Canadian military. In 2002, The TAC-50 made history in the hands of Canada's elite sniper teams.

In March 2002, a five-man sniper team from 3rd Battalion Princess Patricia's Canadian Light Infantry took part in Operation Anaconda in Afghanistan's

▲ In Afghanistan during March 2002, Canadian Army Corporal Robert Furlong used a McMillan TAC-50 similar to this one to record a confirmed kill of a Taliban fighter at a range of 2,430 meters.

Shahi-kot Valley. This operation employed forces from ten allied nations, including the United States, the United Kingdom, Germany, and Afghan militia fighters, in an effort to destroy a large concentration of Al Qaeda and Taliban fighters reported to have assembled in the valley.

The Canadian snipers were attached to the US Army's 187th Infantry Regiment. On March 2, 2002, this force was assigned to sweep the Shahi-kot Valley to root out enemy forces in the area. During this operation, Master Corporal Arron Perry used his McMillan TAC-50 to kill a Taliban fighter at a distance of 2,310 meters (2,526 yards), which topped Marine Gunnery Sergeant Carlos Hathcock's thirty-five-year-old record by 24 meters. Only a few days later, Perry's teammate, Corporal Robert Furlong, broke Perry's record when he shot a Taliban fighter carrying a Soviet RPK machine gun at a distance of 2,430 meters (2,657 yards). Like Perry, Furlong used a McMillan TAC-50 to make his kill shot.

Seven years later in 2009, a British Army soldier, Corporal of Horse Craig Harrison of the Royal Horse Guards, broke Furlong's record. Using an Accuracy International L115A3 bolt-action rifle chambered for .338 Lapua, he killed two Taliban machine gunners in consecutive shots at 2,475 meters (2,707 yards). Harrison and his spotter needed nine shots to get the range before delivering the kill shots.

At a media event sponsored by McMillan, I had a brief opportunity to shoot the TAC-50. Unfortunately, I did not get to shoot a bench rest group, but I am one of very few who has shot one off-hand. I was impressed by the TAC-50's quality of workmanship and the smooth and solid lock-up of the action. The muzzle brake was very efficient, which made shooting it off-hand a pleasant experience–at least as pleasant as trying to heft and shoot a 26-pound rifle plus scope can be.

A better proof of the moderate recoil of a TAC-50 was demonstrated that day when a fairly petite young

▲ The author, a lefty, shoots a McMillan TAC-50 at a range near Phoenix, Arizona. Note the detachable magazine. The scope is a tactical variable with a side parallax adjustment by Schmidt & Bender.

lady shot the TAC-50 several times from the prone position. Remarkably, she had never before fired a gun, but sat up smiling after firing the TAC-50.

In 2012, McMillan introduced the TAC-50A1-R2, which is equipped with a new hydraulic recoil mitigation system. Based on my experience shooting the TAC-50, this might be gilding the lily a bit. However, there must be a demand or McMillan wouldn't have offered it. I haven't tried it, but it must be a real pussy cat.

It isn't surprising that the TAC-50 has a price tag that reflects the high quality that McMillan rifles are famous for. Unfortunately, that puts the TAC-50 well out of my financial reach.

However, other more moderately priced options exist for we who are fiscally challenged.

ArmaLite AR-50

In fact there are a number of moderately priced .50 BMG rifle options, such as the Ferret 50 and the LAR Grizzly. Both have good track records, but, in my opinion, some drawbacks as well. So, I turned my eye toward ArmaLite, Inc.

The ArmaLite AR-50 has an octagonal bolt-action that nestles into a vee-shaped recess in a solid aluminum stock. A T-slotted accessory groove runs the full length of the forestock. From muzzle to butt pad, the AR-50 measures 58.5 inches and weighs 34.1 pounds.

The 30-inch, 8-groove, chrome-moly barrel is fully floated and has a 1–in-15 twist. The massive muzzle brake looks like it came off a tank cannon and reduces recoil to about what you'd expect from a .308 Winchester.

Both the buttplate and the steel cheek piece are vertically adjustable on a skeletonized buttstock. The cheek piece is made of heavy-gauge sheet steel that curves to a right angle, presenting a comfortable cheek rest to a right-handed shooter. However, if you try to shoot left-handed, the cheek piece presents a blunt one-eighth-inch edge to your cheek. Since I'm a southpaw, this looked like a deal-breaker.

Fortunately, ArmaLite decided to manufacture a limited run of a left-hand .50 BMG rifle and designated it the AR-50L. I wasted no time putting in my order for one, and it soon arrived at my local FFL dealer.

When it arrived, it needed a few things before taking it to the range. I installed a Sinclair folding bipod using a sling swivel stud adapter in the forestock accessory groove. I also swapped the existing picatinny rail for one with a 20-minute forward tilt and mounted a Leupold VX-3, 6.5-20x50mm LR riflescope with a Varmint Hunter reticle on my AR-50L.

▲ The author shoots his left-hand Armalite AR50L chambered for .50 BMG from a bench rest. His scope is a Leupold VX3 6.5-20x50 LR, which has a ballistic reticle that he prefers over the usual mil-dot. *Photo credit: Tyler Hartung*

My first trip to the firing range was successful. Using the Sinclair bipod on a sturdy shooting table, My AR-50L exhibited outstanding accuracy at 1,000, even with M33 ball ammo, which they say, is designed to deliver a cone of fire, rather than a tight group. The range trip also revealed one more item that I found to be essential—a carry handle.

Trying to lug a nearly 5-foot, 35-pound rifle up a steep berm to a shooting table is not easy. There's no ready handhold except the riflescope, and that's a no-no. Fortunately, ArmaLite offers a carry handle that provides a convenient grip near the AR-50's balance point. It's fairly pricy at $150, but don't leave home without one.

An accurate rifle chambered for .50 BMG or a similar long-range cartridge is essential for shooting beyond 1,000 yards. You also need good ballistic data; a laser rangefinder, or other accurate means of determining range; and "met data" (altitude, temperature, humidity, wind, coriolis effect—and maybe a ballistic calculator to compute a firing solution from all this data).

But all this is useless without a stable platform from which to shoot. Under field conditions, a solid shooting bench is rarely available, and shooting prone off a bipod works only some of the time. I wanted something more for my AR-50L, and by chance the ideal solution appeared.

An old gun nut buddy of mine emailed me about a website that was selling anti-aircraft tripods for the German MG42. I checked it out and found a vastly over-engineered German device with robust legs that could be splayed out to shoot from about a foot off the ground or cinched in to provide a shooting platform nearly six feet high to facilitate firing the MG42 at aircraft almost directly overhead. The telescoping legs could adjust to provide solid support in almost any terrain.

It was obviously sturdy enough. All I needed was to modify the attachment to mount my AR-50L.

▲ Tyler Hartung fires the author's .50 BMG AR-50L from a German M42 anti-aircraft tripod that the author and Tucson gun enthusiast Mike Strong modified to accept the 35-pound rifle.

Another friend of mine is a skilled machinist, and with his help I had a one-of-a-kind platform that would allow me to shoot my AR-50L accurately from any stance—including standing. We also devised a turnbuckle-style mechanism that controlled elevation and gave a rock-steady, additional point of support.

ArmaLite now makes an upgraded AR-50 designated the AR-50A1. It is available in several configurations, including a National Match model with a three-inch longer barrel and specially selected component parts. It is guaranteed to shoot sub-MOA groups.

As for me, I am happy with my AR-50L. Since only a few of them were made, it should be very collectible in years to come. If it were a repeater with a detachable box magazine, I'd be ecstatic. However, it ain't bad just as it is.

VIII. Machine Guns

*I*n 1862, the hand-cranked, multi-barreled Gatling gun was patented. Adopted by the US military and later by the British, it performed with distinction in many wars and insurrections on several continents. However, it required constant muscle power and several soldiers to operate it in battle.

Hiram Maxim Breaks New Ground

In 1884, Hiram Maxim patented his recoil-operated, belt-fed machine gun. For the first time, a machine gun could operate without muscle power to turn a crank. This meant a much higher rate of fire, limited only by barrel heating. Operator fatigue was reduced to almost nothing, and it was possible to aim a recoil-operated gun with a fair degree of accuracy.

Maxim made one other contribution to the development of machine guns. To counteract extreme barrel heating from a 600-round-per-minute rate of fire, Maxim invented a water-filled jacket surrounding the barrel to provide evaporative cooling. This proved effective, permitting extended bursts of fire; and it was incorporated into the design of the Maxim gun.

Maxim Goes into Business

Maxim founded the Maxim Gun Company in London, England to produce his machine gun. It was financed by Albert Vickers, who became company chairman. A prototype accompanied the Emin Pasha Relief Expedition in Africa. This expedition was led by African explorer Henry Morton Stanley, and the Maxim was used on several occasions to ward off attackers. Several countries, including Germany, obtained manufacturing licenses, and the Maxim gun was adopted for use by armies throughout Europe.

Then in 1888, General Sir Garnet Wolseley, who was commander in chief of the British Army, ordered the purchase of Maxim machine guns for the army. They were chambered for the British Army's standard rifle cartridge, the .577-400 Martini-Henry.

Maxim machine guns fought with the British Army in several wars and insurrections, including the Mahdist rebellion, both Matabele wars, and both Boer wars.

Enter John M. Browning

In the fall of 1889, the news of Maxim's machine gun had not spread to such remote communities as Ogden, Utah, where three Browning brothers were watching the Ogden Gun Club's weekly shoot, waiting for their turn at the firing line. The brothers had undoubtedly heard of the Gatling gun, but none of them had ever seen one.

The Gatling gun was far from their thoughts, however, as they watched a good friend, Will Wright, take aim at the target with his single-shot Browning rifle. Then something remarkable happened that would alter the course of warfare for the next century and more:

Will fired at his target and a patch of weeds about ten feet in front of the muzzle was blown flat by the muzzle blast. That was not the remarkable thing. Weeds being blown around by a rifle's muzzle blast was a common occurrence that had happened countless times on this and other shooting ranges throughout the world.

The blowing weeds, of course, were not remarkable. What *was* remarkable was the effect on John M. Browning. Like everyone else present, John Browning had seen the blowing weeds countless times, but this time it sparked an idea. It took energy from the rifle shot to blow those weeds around—wasted energy—energy that could be used to work a rifle mechanism.

It was an epiphany.

John Browning collected his brothers and left the firing range. By the next afternoon, the Browning brothers had assembled a working prototype of a gas-operated automatic rifle.

More important, it was not a recoil-operated mechanism like the Maxim. It was a completely new principle. John Browning, assisted by his brothers Matt and Ed, had invented a *gas-operated* full-automatic rifle. On January 6, 1890, John M. Browning filed the first patent for the gas-operating principle.

Scarcely a year later, Browning visited the Colt's Patent Manufacturing Co. in Hartford, Connecticut, and demonstrated his shop prototype machine gun, which fired 200 rounds continuously without a

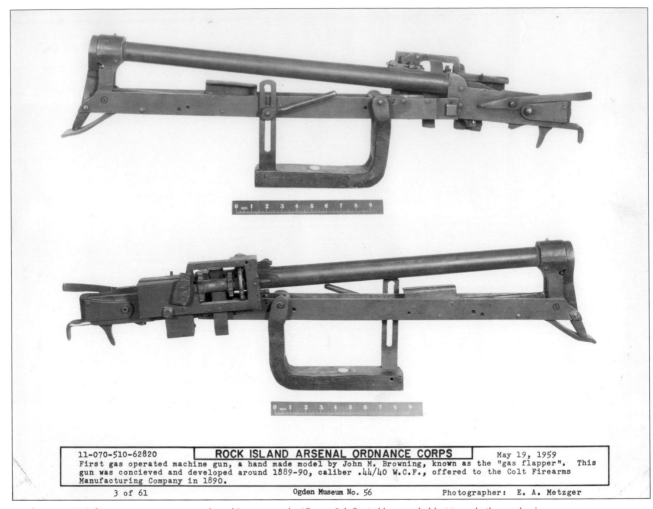

▲ John Browning's first prototype gas-operated machine gun used a "flapper" deflected by muzzle blast to cycle the mechanism.
Photo courtesy of Browning Arms

◀ John Browning with his Model 1895 "Potato Digger" machine gun, which was manufactured by Colt. The M1895 saw limited use by the US Navy and several Latin American countries. Two M1895s supported the Rough Riders during the Battle of San Juan Heights.
Photo courtesy of Browning Arms

stoppage. In an unofficial demonstration for US Naval Ordnance officers several months later, the Browning prototype fired 2,000 rounds continuously without a single stoppage despite a fine mist of lead that permeated the air. The barrel glowed red before the demonstration ended.

By the end of 1894, Browning had filed six patents on gas-operated mechanisms, and in the following year, Colt had begun producing what came to be known as the Colt Model 1895 Automatic Machine Gun, later nicknamed "Potato-Digger" for its underslung toggle mechanism. These were chambered for the .30-40 Krag and 6mm Lee Navy cartridges. The Navy ordered 50 M1895s, and Colt sold a fair number to various Latin American countries. Two privately owned Colt M1895s in .30-40 Krag augmented Lieutenant Parker's Gatlings at the Battle of San Juan Heights during the Spanish-American War.

Preparations for War

The Maxim Gun Company was absorbed by the Vickers Company in 1896. In due course, Vickers redesigned the Maxim, making several improvements, and the new Vickers machine gun, chambered for the .303 British rifle cartridge, was adopted by the British Army in 1912.

In Germany, a Maxim variant, the *Maschinengewehr 08*, was adopted in 1908; and two years later, Russia adopted a Maxim variant, the *Pulemyot Maxima M10*, for use by the Imperial Russian Army.

▼ The *Pulemyot Maxima M10*, a variant of the Maxim machine gun, was adopted in 1910 for use by the Imperial Russian Army. It is only one of the many kinds of machine guns you'll find on the firing line at the Big Sandy Machine Gun Shoot near Wikieup, Arizona.

Wholesale Slaughter Looms on the Horizon

Several other countries, including France, Italy, and the Ottoman Empire had adopted the Maxim or a variant. The armies of virtually all European nations were now armed with machine guns, but military tactics in all Armies lagged far behind this new battlefield technology. This tragic fact would cause combat casualties on a scale not dreamed of in nineteenth century warfare. Sixteen million soldiers on all sides were killed and more than 20 million were wounded from 1914 to 1918. A major portion of those casualties occurred during massed frontal assaults on prepared trench positions bristling with heavy machine guns.

The Changing Face of Warfare

Toward the end of World War I, numerous automatic weapon designs appeared, and here are a few of the best. Three of them were designed by John Moses Browning. If this seems like a pro-Browning tilt, remember this is *my* opinion about which are the best—so sue me.

Browning Model 1917 Water-Cooled Machine Gun

John Browning began working on a new machine gun in 1900, realizing that the Colt M1895 he had designed was outdated. He reasoned that the United States would eventually begin trials for a replacement.

◀ During an initial test of John Browning's M1917 water-cooled machine gun at Springfield Armory Proving Ground, it fired 20,000 rounds without a stoppage. Browning then ordered another 20,000 rounds to be fired—again, no stoppages.
Photo courtesy of Browning Arms

He told his brothers, "It would make me pretty hot to have a foreign gun come over here and steal a big order while I was taking a nap."

He had already figured out the design and had the new gun finished and firing in about three months. Throughout the years, Browning tweaked and modified the new gun, changing it to eject from the bottom instead of the side and increasing the rate of fire.

A test of the Browning machine gun took place at the Springfield Armory proving ground in May 1917. During this test 20,000 rounds were fired without any malfunctions or broken parts. Browning then decided to increase the stakes and fired another 20,000 rounds flawlessly. By August of that year, the government issued the first production contracts for the new machine gun, and it was designated the Browning Model 1917 .30 Caliber Water Cooled Machine Gun.

This design spawned several variations, including an air-cooled aircraft machine gun, a tank-mounted machine gun, and air-cooled light machine guns.

The M1917 Browning and its variations served America in four wars spanning nearly six decades, and may still be found in armed conflicts around the world.

The .30 caliber Browning light and heavy machine guns are some of the most popular Class III weapons at the many machine gun shoots around the country. Many of them have been modified to accept the current US service cartridge (7.62x51mm NATO) to take advantage of still-plentiful and relatively cheap surplus ammo.

▼ Not all shooters at the Big Sandy Machine Gun Shoot are men. This young lady is playing a tune on a Soviet-era RPD light machine gun, which was designed in 1944, but was not produced in large numbers until 1953. It is chambered for 7.62x39mm, the same cartridge used by the AK-47.

My favorite is still the Model 1917 Water Cooled, which today has a price tag hovering near $20,000 for one in decent condition. For a gun nut like me whose heart goes aflutter at the night shoots at Big Sandy, the M1917 offers an easily maintained, reliable machine gun that will spew tracers into the night as long as my wallet will allow me to hold the trigger back.

Browning Automatic Rifle

Long before World War I began, the US Army Ordnance Corps had expressed a need for a weapon that could provide an individual soldier the capability for "walking fire." Certain that America would be drawn into WWI, John Browning began to work on an automatic rifle expressly designed for that purpose. Then, when the army scheduled a live fire demonstration in February 1917, he brought his automatic rifle with him along with the water-cooled machine gun he had been perfecting for the best part of two decades.

The demonstration of the automatic rifle before three hundred congressmen, high-ranking military officials and other observers was so impressive that Browning received a contract for the new weapon within days. The water-cooled machine gun underwent further testing before its adoption.

Designated the Model 1918 Browning Automatic Rifle, it went into combat late in WWI and played a significant role in the Meuse-Argonne offensive. It served the US military as a squad automatic rifle until 1958.

After the war, Colt obtained the Browning patents and offered the BAR for commercial sale, but it generated little public interest. Famous exhibition shooter Ad Topperwein obtained a BAR and astonished audiences by shooting small, hand-thrown steel discs out of the air.

By the 1930s, gangsters such as Clyde Barrow and Bonnie Parker, better known as Bonnie and Clyde, used the BAR, although they burglarized National

▼ The author smokes a target at 200 yards with a Browning Automatic Rifle, better known as the BAR—one of John M. Browning's most successful designs. Photo credit: J. D. Jones

▲ Shooting the M1918 Browning Automatic Rifle, or BAR, is pure fun as indicated by the author's ear-to-ear grin. *Photo credit: J. D. Jones*

Guard Armories from time to time for their weapons and ammo. Contemporary accounts indicate Clyde taught Bonnie to operate the BAR, and she became fairly accomplished with it.

My personal experience with the BAR is limited, but contrary to stories about it being a difficult weapon to master, I found it to have a mild recoil, probably because its 17-pound weight contributed to stability. That's a good trade—much better than a lightweight weapon with punishing recoil. Remember, a full-auto shoulder weapon hits you with recoil several times per second, instead of a bolt-action rifle's once.

I found the BAR to be very controllable, and it was very easy to keep rounds on target as far away as 300 to 400 yards. The BAR is now one of my favorites and near the top of my wish list.

Lewis Gun

Automatic weapons designed by Americans dominated the battlefield throughout World War I and afterward. Among these inventors were Hiram Maxim, John M. Browning and Brigadier General John T. Thompson; but there was one more American inventor

of automatic weapons—Colonel Isaac Newton Lewis, who invented the versatile Lewis gun.

With its distinctive horizontal pan magazine and its bulky-looking barrel cooling shroud, the Lewis gun stood apart from other automatic weapons of its era. The Lewis gun could accept both a 47-round and a 97-round magazine. Unlike the drum magazine of the Thompson submachine gun (and others), the Lewis magazine was not spring-wound. Instead it used a mechanical cam and pawl mechanism that made it simpler to reload and much more reliable.

The cooling shroud was purported to use muzzle blast to draw cooling air past the barrel, with questionable results. In fact, the cooling shroud was omitted on most aircraft and anti-aircraft variations.

During World War I, the Lewis gun was manufactured in the .303 British cartridge by Birmingham Small Arms (BSA) in England and in both the .30-06 Springfield cartridge and .303 British by Savage Arms in the U.S. Germany rebarreled captured Lewis guns in 7.92x57mm and used them both in WWI and WWII.

By 1916, the 28-pound Lewis gun replaced the much heavier Vickers machine gun in British front-line combat units, and aircraft-mounted Lewis guns were used by British, American, and French forces.

By WWII, the British army had adopted the Bren gun to replace the Lewis gun, but was still the standard close-range air defense weapon of the Royal Navy. It was also used as an anti-aircraft gun for airfield defense and by British Home Guard units. The US Army never adopted the Lewis gun for infantry use, but Merchant Marine and US Coast Guard vessels were equipped with the Lewis gun.

When I laid my hands on a Lewis gun for the first time, it looked as awkward and unwieldy as I had anticipated it would. That impression lasted only as long as it took me to fire a short burst into a derelict washing machine 300 yards downrange. The trigger was a good one, and it allowed me to easily control the length of my short bursts, which is considered to be the most effective technique for combat fire support. Finally, my host, J. D. Jones, told me to just hold the trigger back until the drum was empty. I did so and was surprised to find it easy to keep the long, sustained burst centered on the old washing machine.

Suddenly, I had a new addition to my list of Class III favorites.

Comparing the Lewis gun with my other favorite, the BAR, I found that, in comparison, each had its strong points and weak points. First of all, there's weight—depending on which variation, the BAR weighs around 17 pounds, and the Lewis gun weighs in at 28 pounds in its most common version. The BAR, obviously, is a lot easier to carry than the Lewis gun. But the BAR was designed for "walking fire" as the shooter advanced in the attack, and the Lewis gun was intended to be fired from a bipod, supporting an attack or laying down defensive fire. In this role, the extra weight would provide additional stability for accurate fire.

The second obvious difference is magazine capacity. The relatively compact 20-round magazines used by the BAR are readily carried in belt or vest pouches and a trained operator can switch them in a matter of two or three seconds. This is useful to an automatic rifleman moving forward in the attack. On the other hand, the Lewis gun's large pan (or drum) magazines are cumbersome to carry and switch out when empty. But these drums hold either 47 rounds or 97 rounds, which is more than twice the capacity or nearly five times, respectively, the capacity of a BAR 20-round magazine.

Of course, each could be (and were) used effectively in either role, so in the final analysis, both the Lewis and the BAR score high in versatility. So, which ranks higher in my book?

I don't know. I'm still trying to figure that out.

Ma Deuce

In 1917, General John J. Pershing (later General of the Armies) asked the US Army Ordnance Department for a vastly more powerful machine gun. He wanted it to be at least .50 caliber, shooting 670-grain bullet at 2,700 fps. This was well beyond the capabilities of any machine gun/cartridge combination that existed at the time.

When the Ordnance Department went to the Colt offices in Hartford, Connecticut, to ask John M. Browning whether he could build such a gun, Browning replied, ". . . you make up some cartridges, and we'll go shoot."

Winchester was given the task to develop the new cartridge, which they did by simply scaling up the .30-06 Springfield to .50 caliber. The new cartridge easily fulfilled General Pershing's requirements, and it was named the .50 caliber Browning Machine Gun (.50 BMG). By the time a sample lot of .50 BMG had arrived at the Colt's manufacturing facility, John Browning was already assembling a water-cooled machine gun that would fire the new cartridge. This new gun was very similar to the .30 caliber M1917 Browning already in service. The main difference was an oil buffer that provided a means of controlling the rate of fire while reducing the strain of heavy recoil on the internal parts.

The new machine gun was test-fired successfully, and a government test was scheduled for November 11, 1918, at Aberdeen Proving Ground. When the Armistice ending the war was signed on that day, the test was postponed for four days. John Browning handled the gun himself during the test, firing nearly 900 rounds in 100- to 150-round bursts with no malfunctions.

However, with the end of the war, the water-cooled Browning .50 caliber machine gun was not adopted into service.

▲ The Browning M2 .50 caliber machine gun, affectionately known as Ma Deuce, makes powerful medicine at the Big Sandy Machine Gun Shoot near Wikieup, Arizona.

Much later, the .50-caliber Browning was converted to a much lighter-weight, heavy-barreled, air-cooled model that was accepted by the US Army in 1933. This model, designated the M2, was probably the most effective aircraft-mounted armament of World War II. The B-17 flying fortress that devastated Germany in multi-hundred plane daylight bombing raids carried as many as thirteen Browning .50 caliber machine guns. American fighter aircraft such as the Republic P-47 and North American P-51, were armed with eight Browning .50 caliber machine guns. The standard load was 27 feet of linked .50 BMG armor-piercing and tracer ammo for each machine gun. As we previously discussed, this led to the slang expression *the whole nine yards*, which is used even today and means to give it all you have.

The Browning M2 .50 caliber machine gun was also used as a turret-mounted weapon on the M4 Sherman medium tank and is still used in this role even today on the M1 Abrams main battle tank. The M2 is used on armored personnel carriers, many self-propelled artillery pieces, and various scout vehicles. Equipped with a tripod, the M2 is also effective in fortified defensive positions.

Affectionately called the Ma Deuce, the Browning M2 .50-caliber machine gun has served the US military for eighty years, second only to the M1911/M1911 A1 service pistol, which was also designed by John Browning. Both firearms are still in service, although the M1911 A1 is limited-issue for certain special operations units.

At civilian machine gun shoots such as Knob Creek and Big Sandy, the thundering roar of a Ma Deuce is a familiar sound. Oddly enough, a Browning M2 can often be purchased for about the same price as many less awesome machine guns. You have to remember, though, the least expensive linked .50 BMG ammo costs around $250 per 100 rounds. That's what a 10-second burst from a Ma Deuce will cost you.

▲ Kenton Tucker, one of the organizers of the Big Sandy Machine Gun Shoot, has little to fear from his zombie passengers with his jeep-mounted Ma Deuce and Browning M1917 water-cooled machine gun close by. If that is not enough firepower, the Browning BAR on a rack by the steering wheel is ready and available.

German MG 42

The iconic *Maschinengewehr 42* was the workhorse machine gun of the German Wehrmacht from its introduction in 1942 until VE Day in 1945. It replaced the earlier MG 34, being easier and cheaper to produce than the earlier gun. It was also more reliable with fewer stoppages.

Two notable features made the MG 42 stand out from other machine guns of the time, and one or both of these features made it probably the best machine gun of the war.

The first and most obvious feature was its high cyclic rate (rate of fire), which was 1,200 rounds per minute. The terrifying psychological effect it had on opposing troops led the US Army to produce a training film designed to help soldiers cope with facing an MG 42. The reasoning behind this high rate of fire was that a gunner would have a very short window of time to fire at the enemy; therefore,

it was best to fire as many bullets as possible. Nevertheless, the MG 42's high rate of fire could be its greatest drawback.

The second feature was the MG 42's quick-change barrel. None of the opposing armies' machine guns had such a feature, but on the MG 42, it was indispensable because of rapid barrel heating from a sustained burst at 1,200 rpm.

Employing an MG 42 in combat was not a trivial matter. A German heavy machine gun squad (which served one MG 42) had seven members, a squad leader, gunner, assistant gunner, three rifleman/bearers (who carried a tripod for the MG 42, ammo, spare barrels, and other equipment) and, sometimes, a horseman who handled a horse and cart.

A light machine gun team consisted of a gunner, loader and spotter. In this case, the MG 42 was usually equipped with a bipod replacing the heavy tripod, which gave the team greater mobility.

Despite the psychological effect, the MG 42 could consume ammo at an alarming rate. To make the logistics problem worse, German battle doctrine called for considerably more machine guns than Allied doctrine, which centered on the individual rifleman.

Ironically, the Handbook of the German Army bowed to this logistics reality by forbidding more than a 250-round burst of fire and mandated sustained fire rate not to exceed 300 to 350 rounds per minute. So, after designing the MG 42 to have a high rate of fire, they trained their machine gunners to slow it down.

After the war, the MG 42 continued to serve in the armies of several European countries. Several improved variations appeared, including some chambered for 7.62x51mm NATO for members of that alliance. Some of these are still in use today, including the Beretta MG 42/59 used by the Italian army and the Rheinmetall MG3 of the present-day German *Bundeswehr*.

The MG 42 is fairly popular among American collectors and shooters. Certainly its history, mystique and the ripping sound when an MG 42 fires usually draw many admirers at Class III shows and shooting events.

IX. Gatling Guns To Miniguns

When Dr. Richard Gatling patented his hand-cranked, multi-barreled machine gun in 1862, he saw it as a way to reduce battlefield deaths from combat and disease. He reasoned that because it could fire at a rate equal to as many as fifty trained soldiers, it would reduce the size of armies and, therefore, reduce the number of soldiers at risk of dying.

Gatling versus Gardner

The Gardner gun, invented by William Gardner, followed in 1874. Both of these designs were limited by operator fatigue when turning the crank for extended periods. The cranking motion also interfered with aiming the gun precisely.

Despite these drawbacks, both of these designs played a part in major wars. The Gatling gun, of course, was used sparingly during the Civil War (War Between the States, for those of you with a Confederate bent). It also played a key role at the Battle of San Juan Hill during the Spanish-American War.

Gatling Guns at San Juan Heights

First Lieutenant John Henry Parker (later Brigadier General) commanded the V Corps Gatling Gun Detachment of four 10-barreled Gatling guns chambered for the .30-40 service cartridge. Lt. Parker emplaced three of these guns in support of the assault on Kettle Hill (part of the San Juan Heights) by Lieutenant Colonel Theodore Roosevelt's Rough Riders.

▼ Shining brightly in the Arizona sun, a Gatling gun (left) and a Gardner gun are ready to rock 'n' roll at the Big Sandy Machine Gun Shoot.

▲ This Model 1895 Gatling gun, on display at the NRA's Whittington Center, was recovered from Bannerman Island Arsenal in New York in a condition "best described as junk. . ." and painstakingly restored. It is similar to those Gatlings used in the Spanish-American War and might actually have seen service in that war.

During the Rough Riders' assault, the Gatling guns raked the Spanish trenches on the crest of the hill, killing many of the enemy and causing others to flee in disorder. After the Rough Riders took the hill, Trooper Jesse D. Langdon of the 1st Volunteer Infantry credited the Gatling guns with the victory. He said:

"We were exposed to the Spanish fire, but there was very little because just before we started, why, the Gatling guns opened up at the bottom of the hill, and everybody yelled, "The Gatlings! The Gatlings!" and away we went. The Gatlings just enfiladed the top of those trenches. We'd never have been able to take Kettle Hill if it hadn't been for Parker's Gatling guns."

Colonel Roosevelt also gave the Gatling guns much of the credit for the successful assault and praised Lt. Parker's good judgment and foresight in placing the guns where they could support the attack.

Lieutenant Parker and his Gatlings weren't finished, though. The next day, Parker placed two of his Gatlings in support of the Rough Riders who were preparing to repulse a counterattack. The Spanish did counterattack, sending six hundred troops to retake Kettle Hill. Lieutenant Parker ordered one of the Gatlings to fire into the flank of the attacking infantry at a range of 600 yards. The Gatling opened up, killing more than five hundred Spanish troops and sending the rest into a disordered retreat.

Dr. Gatling tested the M1893 Gatling gun with an electric motor-powered belt drive to replace the hand crank. These tests showed that the Gatling could fire bursts at 1,500 rpm, but an electric motor powered gun was not practical for field use. Also the high rate of fire was not seen to offer a tactical advantage over a hand-cranked Gatling.

Various models of the Gatling gun remained in active service with the US Army until 1909 when they were replaced by the M1909 Benet-Mercie machine gun.

▲ The Gardner gun on the firing line at the Big Sandy Machine Gun Shoot shows its distinctive side-by-side barrel configuration.

Gardner Gun at War

Having been adopted by the British Army, the Gardner gun accompanied the British Gordon Relief Expedition during the Mahdist Rebellion in the Sudan. This force was sent to Khartoum in late December 1884 to rescue General Charles "Chinese" Gordon and the remnants of Egyptian troops besieged by the Mahdi Army. In a pitched battle at *Abu Klea*, the Gardner guns proved almost useless in the desert conditions of blowing sand and dust.

The Bira Gun

As westerners, we often overlook the ingenuity and technological skills of eastern cultures. So, it might come as a surprise that in the mid-1890s, the Kingdom of Nepal produced an independently designed, hand-cranked machine gun similar in function to the Gardner gun of the 1860s.

Nepal, famous for the fierce Gurkha fighters who served the British with distinction in many wars across the globe, was well-supplied with arms and ammunition by the British, but they were reluctant to include machine guns in the mix. So the Nepalese decided to design and produce their own.

They turned to one of their best military engineers, General Gahendra Shamsher Jang Bahadur Rana, to design the gun. Lacking the precision machining resources to manufacture a fully automatic machine gun, it was decided that a crank-operated machine gun similar to the American Gardner gun would be suitable. It would be chambered for the .577-450 British Martini-Henry cartridge that Nepal had stockpiled in huge quantities.

▲ The Bira gun data plate credits General Gahendra, Nepalese Military Engineers (in English), as its inventor. The remainder is in Nepali, the official language of Nepal.

The Bira gun was completely handmade and weighed about 1,000 pounds on its artillery carriage with spoked, teak wheels. Very few parts were interchangeable, if any. It was fed from a 120-round drum magazine that weighed 40 pounds loaded. These were numbered to the individual gun, so interchangeability was iffy, at best.

The crank was pulled backward, toward the operator, which Gahendra believed was more natural and less fatiguing. After a range session with his Bira gun, arms historian Garry James said, "I can't say I disagree with him."

James described his Bira as ". . . a fairly efficient contrivance, assuming all things are properly timed, adjusted and well-lubricated." At the range, James's Bira gun was fired at some jugs filled with colored water. It malfunctioned a few times, which was attrib-

uted to a broken spring, but at the end of the day, no jugs were left standing.

James's gun is one of a small batch that was imported by Interarms in association with Val Forgett of Navy Arms. A few of these are still available through International Military Antiques (www.ima.com) and Atlanta Cutlery (www.atlantacutlery.com). A collector can own one of them at a fraction of the cost of a vintage Gatling gun.

The Maxim machine gun had been invented in 1884, so the Bira gun was already hopelessly obsolete when it appeared in the mid-1990s. Still, as a completely independent design, it demonstrated the ingenuity of eastern engineering technology. There is no record of the Bira gun actually being used in battle, so it remains merely an interesting footnote in military weaponry.

▲ Arms historian Garry James wipes down his Nepalese Bira gun. Note the twin barrels and the horizontal pan magazine. The magazine holds 120 rounds of .577-450 Martini-Henry ammo in two rows of 60.

A New Lease on Life

In 1911, the Army declared the Gatling gun obsolete, and the Gatling era appeared to be over after nearly fifty years of service. It wasn't until 1946 when the US government issued a contract to General Electric to develop a multi-barreled aircraft cannon. Originally designed for a 15mm explosive round, the cannon eventually evolved into a 20mm weapon with a 6,000 round-per-minute rate of fire. This was adopted in 1959 as the M61 Vulcan and installed as the principal armament in the F-104A Starfighter. The M61 later became the standard gun for most subsequent US fighter aircraft, including a lighter version in the F-22 Raptor stealth fighter.

During the Vietnam War, a requirement emerged for a 7.62x51mm rotary gun for Army gunship helicopters. The government again turned to General Electric, who designed the GAU-2B/A Minigun. The Minigun was electrically operated, and its six rotating barrels fired at a cyclic rate of 3,000 rpm. Designated by the army as the M134, the Minigun was employed successfully in the Vietnam War in helicopter gunships, including the revolutionary Bell AH-1 HueyCobra. It also gained a fearsome reputation in the AC-47, which was a converted cargo aircraft. The AC-47, sporting three

▲ This Bira gun, owned by firearms historian Garry James, was manufactured in Nepal and chambered for the .577/450 Martini-Henry cartridge. It was designed by General Gahendra Shamsher Jang Bahadur Rana, a Nepalese military engineer.

Miniguns that fired out the left side of the fuselage, became known as "Puff The Magic Dragon." Puff's three Miniguns could deliver a devastating cloud of fire to an elliptical beaten zone approximately 47.5 meters in size. A three-second burst could place at least one 7.62mm projectile in every square meter within the beaten zone.

Following the Vietnam War, the Minigun fell into disuse, suffering from uncorrected design flaws, shortage of spare parts and inadequate product support. By the mid-1990s, the Minigun was close to retirement. That's when Dillon Aero came to its rescue with a redesigned feeder/delinker, which was adopted by the military. The earlier part had been prone to sudden breakage that required second echelon maintenance to replace.

With the success of the new feeder delinker, Dillon systematically redesigned virtually all of the Minigun's components, creating a vastly improved new generation Minigun.

In 2003, the military adopted the Dillon Minigun as the M134D, replacing the GAU-2B/A as standard. Today, all branches of the US military employ the M134D in a wide variety of roles on the land, sea and air.

Privately Owned Gatling Guns

Collectors and shooters prize original Gatling guns, especially those in shooting condition. Many different

▲ This minigun on the firing line at the Big Sandy Machine Gun Shoot was equipped with double spade handles and an EOTech Holosight. Note the heavy electric cable that powers the minigun's electric motor.

models, some scarcer than others, remain in private hands and occasionally are offered for sale. If you decide you want a Gatling, be advised that even one of the more common models will probably cost you more than a well-kept, spacious home in the suburbs. Even so, vintage Gatlings show up often at machine gun shoots around the country.

At a recent Big Sandy shoot, I saw and photographed a shiny brass, five-barreled Gatling gun alongside an equally shiny brass Gardner gun. They both worked and they both fired at targets during the Big Sandy Shoot.

If you can't summon the low to medium six-figure sum for a vintage Gatling or Gardner gun, take heart. There's another option. It's still an expensive option, but more like the price of a nicely equipped Lexus instead of a few hundred thousand.

How would you like to own a newly manufactured, genuine Colt Model 1877 Bulldog Gatling Gun? Let me say that again—*newly manufactured*—genuine Colt Gatling Gun!

Colt Manufacturing now offers a limited number of special edition Colt Gatling Guns chambered for .45-70. I inspected one that was exhibited at an industry trade show in January 2012. It was a beauty mounted on a massive oak tripod with a gleaming brass barrel shroud. On the top of the breech was a cast brass shield labeling it as a GATLING'S BATTERY GUN made by COLT'S PT. FIRE ARMS MFG CO.

The Colt representative informed me that this gun had been completed only two weeks before the show. Piled on the ground next to the gun were 5,000 fired .45-70 cases, which he told me, had been expended during demonstrations earlier that

▲ The Model 1877 Gatling uses a longitudinal crank to get the job done.

day. The gun could have continued to fire, but they had run out of ammo.

The Colt rep told me that once this edition was sold out, that Colt planned more special editions, including one with a wheeled field carriage.

The price of a new Colt Gatling Gun is well below six figures, but high enough to send this poor boy's hopes aglimmering.

Privately Owned Miniguns

If you crave the ultimate in full-auto firepower instead of simply owning a vintage Gatling gun, a few Miniguns have found their way into collectors' hands. I don't have the figures to back it up, but I suspect that most of these privately owned Miniguns are General Electric/General Dynamics GAU-2B/A models, not Dillon M134Ds.

Now, before you get too excited, here are a few things to think about before you buy one: First, there are prob-ably no more than two or three dozen Miniguns available for civilian ownership. Second, this means that the selling price is climbing steadily. It's already in six figures with some asking prices at more than a quarter million bucks.

Third, pre-Dillon Minigun internal parts have been known to break suddenly, requiring second echelon repairs. This means finding a qualified gunsmith to perform the repair, ordering the necessary replacement part, replacing the broken part. This does not come cheap, but if you own a non-Dillon M134, you'd better put aside a small fund for repairs—you'll need it.

Fourth, the cost of surplus 7.62 NATO has risen dra-matically in the past decade. Even with the cheapest, but decent quality ammo, a Minigun will cost you $1,900 to $2,000 per minute to shoot it.

At a recent Big Sandy Machine Gun Shoot, I watched the owner of a Minigun fire one long burst, then the gun apparently malfunctioned. He and a

▲ This Model 1877 Gatling gun was newly manufactured by Colt in 2012. As the empty brass on the ground shows, it had fired 5,000 rounds of .45-70 ammo in the course of one morning. A Colt representative told me it had been built only two weeks before this demonstration.

▲ This data plate shows that this is not a replica. It is an actual Colt Gatling gun. However, it was manufactured in the twenty-first century, not the nineteenth century.

friend began to work on the gun; but after twenty minutes with no apparent progress, I decided to move on.

About an hour later, I strolled by and noticed the two men still working on the stalled Minigun. I had wanted to get more photos of the Minigun in action, but evidently that would not happen today.

Gatling gun, Gardner gun, and Minigun, each is fascinating in its own way. If I win the lottery, buying one (or more) will be right at the top of my list.

▲ A Minigun chambered for the 7.62x51mm NATO cartridge doing what it does best, chewing up ammo at 4,000 rounds per minute. Put another way, that's $2,000 per minute give or take, depending on how cheaply you can obtain surplus ammo.

X. Field Artillery

Cannon to right of them,
Cannon to left of them,
Cannon in front of them
Volley'd and thunder'd;
Storm'd at with shot and shell,
Boldly they rode and well,
Into the jaws of Death,
Into the mouth of Hell
Rode the six hundred.

—Alfred, Lord Tennyson
"Charge of the Light Brigade"
1854

Revolutionary War Era

By the eighteenth century, cannon fire had become a major component of battle in land warfare. These cannons were of several general types, siege cannons, field cannons, mortars, and howitzers.

Siege cannons were heavy pieces with limited mobility. They were designed to fire solid shot to destroy fortifications and buildings.

Field cannons were relatively light weapons mounted on wheeled carriages, usually drawn by teams of horses. These weapons were designed to fire solid shot, grape shot and canister into enemy infantry formations, tearing great holes in their ranks.

Mortars were considerably different in appearance and purpose. Mounted on a flat bed and elevated by a wooden wedge, mortars were designed to fire an explosive shell in a high trajectory. Flying over breastworks, these shells were intended to explode in the air to rain shrapnel on enemy troops below.

Howitzers were short-barreled weapons usually mounted on wheeled carriages. They were designed for direct fire, like field cannons or at a high trajectory like mortars. However, howitzers did not have the longer range capability of a field cannon and had a much smaller bore than a mortar.

During the Revolutionary War, procedures for aiming and firing an artillery piece were still at a primitive stage and depended greatly on the experience and skill of the gun crew.

A New Century's Artillery Advances

During the first half of the nineteenth century, artillery had begun to evolve, both in equipment and tactics. Massed artillery fire was employed, especially by the Russians who had amassed more artillery pieces than other European armies.

Artillery carriages became lighter, more mobile and capable of more precise aiming. A block trail lightened gun carriages, and the cannons themselves were made with bronze barrels and other design elements that reduced weight almost by half compared to previous designs.

Redesigned limbers allowed gun crews to ride with their cannon and carried a quantity of ready ammunition. This improved mobility and allowed gun crews to unlimber and ready their piece to fire in as little as one minute.

Napoleon Bonaparte placed great emphasis on mobility of his artillery. He adopted especially lightweight cannons that were more than a thousand pounds lighter than contemporary British cannons. He also reorganized his artillery into semi-autonomous formations led by aggressive young officers who turned French artillery into a potent offensive weapon.

Cannons in the Civil War

In the 1860s when the American Civil War began, the smoothbore cannon was still a major force on the battlefield, but advances in metallurgy reduced barrel weight substantially. The practical effect was improved mobility allowing 12-pounder field guns to replace the six-pounders in general battlefield use.

Confederate and Federal armies organized field artillery batteries that were usually composed of four field guns such as the 1857 Napoleon 12-pounder and two howitzers such as the Models 1838 and 1841 field howitzers. Heavier caliber cannons as large as 24- and 32-pounders also saw use, but had limited mobility. Even larger cannons were used in fixed fortifications and on naval warships.

Guns and howitzers differed in several ways. A gun was a long-barreled weapon designed to fire at

▲ On the firing line at the Big Sandy Machine Gun Shoot, the author's ArmaLite AR 50L rests on its tripod next to Mike Strong's Civil War Parrott rifle.

long range using a low-trajectory and a large powder charge. Howitzers had shorter barrels, were usually lighter and had a shorter range than a field gun. Although howitzers were designed for high-angle indirect fire, they were often used for direct fire alongside 12-pounder field guns to repel infantry assaults.

A third type of artillery, the mortar, also was used, ranging from the small Coehorn mortar that could be carried by two men, to huge siege and garrison mortars. The mortar was designed to fire an explosive projectile in a high arcing trajectory over fortifications to explode among troops sheltering behind protective cover.

Rifled Cannons

As the war began, newer types of cannons were being developed. This included rifled muzzleloaders, such as the Parrott rifle, which had a cast iron barrel reinforced with a band of wrought iron. Most Parrott rifles were 10-pounders with a 2.9- or 3-inch bore. However, Parrott rifles as large as 300-pounders were used, notably in the bombardment of Fort Sumter in 1863. The Parrott rifle was very accurate, and a 10-pounder Parrott had maximum range of 1,950 yards.

The rifled bronze James rifle was designed to use a projectile designed by Charles T. James. The James projectile had a lead sabot that would expand to engage the rifling. It was regarded as very accurate, but the soft bronze rifling wore out quickly, and the James rifle soon fell into disfavor.

Also seen were breechloaders such as the Whitworth gun, which had a unique hexagonal bore and a projectile to match. An engineering article of the time claimed that the Whitworth rifle, firing at 1,600 yards had a "lateral deviation of only five inches." This accuracy made it very effective for counterbattery fire.

By the end of the Civil War artillery tactics had evolved to be a decisive and deadly factor in almost every major battle. However, it wasn't until decades later with the development of smokeless propellants and the hydro-pneumatic recoil mechanism, that artillery

had the potential to become the fearsome battlefield weapon that emerged in World War I. But there was one final piece of the puzzle still waiting to fall into place.

Artillery Indirect Fire

Although historical references to indirect artillery fire date back as far as the sixteenth century, virtually all field artillery was used in a direct fire role until the very end of the nineteenth century. NATO defines indirect fire as "fire delivered at a target which cannot be seen by the aimer." The reality of delivering artillery fire *accurately* on a target that can't be seen by the gun crew is far more complex than this simple definition would suggest.

Without going into great detail, here's the problem.

You need someone to see and describe a target and communicate it to the gun or guns (observer). This target is usually miles away behind terrain features and over the horizon.

This information is translated by a fire direction center into instructions on which direction the gun needs to point and how high the tube must be elevated. Further instructions are given on what kind of projectile to use, type of fuse, how it should be set and the propellant charge needed to send the projectile on the correct trajectory to hit the target.

Meanwhile, additional artillery pieces have been designated to perform this fire mission, and these guns are pointed and elevated following the same instructions given to the first gun. But they don't fire yet.

When the first gun is fired, the observer watches for the projectile's impact. If it misses the target, the observer describes how to correct the aim. The fire direction center calculates how to adjust the gun, and all designated guns follow the new pointing and elevating instructions. This might take several shots to put a round on target.

When the next round hits the target, the observer sends a message to "fire for effect." When this happens, all designated guns fire the number of rounds allocated to the fire mission. What happens at the target is a devastating rain of chaos and destruction.

To achieve this result, requires precise aiming equipment, accurate artillery pieces, a reliable means of communication, complex mathematics, and detailed meteorological data. In addition, you need a highly trained observer and gunner as well as fire direction personnel capable of applying higher mathematics.

Besides being able to hit targets the gunner can't see, indirect fire provides one more devastating factor on the modern battlefield. Because it is possible

▶ Setting a friction primer into the Parrott rifle's flash hole is the last step before pulling the lanyard.

◀ A precision rear peep sight made of brass mounts on the right side of the Parrott rifle breech. It is adjustable both for windage and elevation. A fixed front sight is located on the right-side trunnion.

to locate the position of the target according to land-marks or map coordinates, the number of guns that can be concentrated on a single target is limited only by the number of guns available on the battlefield at that moment.

The French 75

Regarded as the first modern artillery piece, the French Model 1897 75mm field gun was used in both World Wars by ten different nations, including the United States, England, and, of course, France. It is still used by several nations to fire ceremonial salutes, and a few are in civilian hands.

The French 75 was the first cannon to use a hydro-pneumatic recoil system. When it was fired, the barrel recoiled, then returned to its "battery" position. This allowed its wheels and trail to remain largely stationary, requiring only minor aiming adjustments between shots. As a result, it was possible to fire the French 75 rapidly

with a great deal of accuracy. Like other cannons at the turn of the nineteenth to twentieth centuries, it was a breechloader and fired fixed ammunition with a brass case. More than 21,000 French 75s were manufactured from 1897 to 1940. Besides its extensive use as a highly mobile field gun, it also was widely employed as an anti-aircraft weapon and even as a tank main gun. The French 75's combination of ruggedness, accuracy, high rate of fire and versatility established the pattern for most new artillery designs even today.

Deadly Artillery Tactics

In World War I, the number of guns used in a battle could be in the hundreds. In a few major battles, the number was in the thousands. Trench warfare along with indirect fire by massed artillery spawned a new phenomenon—the artillery barrage.

An artillery barrage was a form of planned fire. It could be used to concentrate artillery fire on a small

► Shaped like a pellet for an air rifle, the five-pound Parrott rifle projectile has a hollow skirt that, upon ignition of the powder charge, expands to engage the rifling.

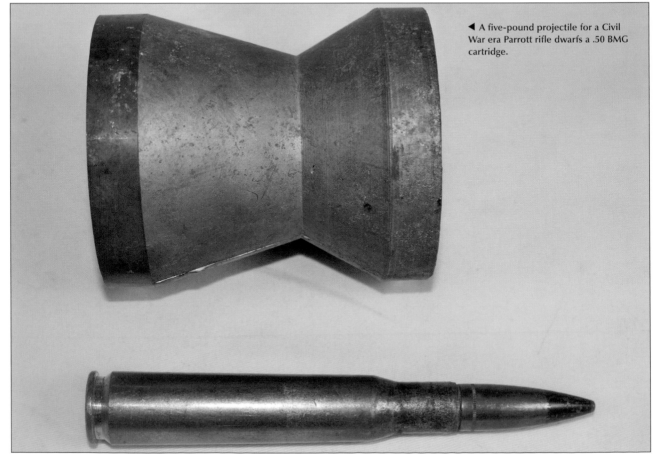

◄ A five-pound projectile for a Civil War era Parrott rifle dwarfs a .50 BMG cartridge.

area, but it could take other, sometimes complex forms. One of the most commonly used was the "walking" or "rolling" barrage.

A walking barrage placed fire in a line blanketing an area of a few hundred yards just in front of friendly trenches. This barrage would move or "walk" slowly toward the enemy trenches with an attacking wave of troops just behind it, thus suppressing enemy defensive fire during the advance.

Just before the attacking troops reached the enemy trenches the barrage would be lifted. Then, the attacking wave would fall upon the enemy, who it was hoped, would be dead or still stunned by the ferocity of the barrage.

In conjunction with the walking barrage, a standing barrage was sometimes used a short distance farther back behind the enemy defensive line. This was designed to prevent enemy troops and equipment from reinforcing the front line or counter-attacking.

Tactics such as these caused World War I combat casualties to rise to shocking levels never before seen in warfare. Among all combatants in World War I, nearly 10 million military personnel were killed in combat and more than 22 million were wounded. Roughly 70 percent of all these casualties were the result of artillery fire.

Artillery Evolution

Between the two World Wars, artillery of all kinds evolved at a rapid pace. Field artillery became more mobile with longer range, and guns as large as 155mm and even higher played an increasing role.

Battleship main guns increased in caliber to 16 inches and even 18 inches on World War II Japanese behemoths. As radar directed main guns on battleships made over-the-horizon naval battles possible, they became suddenly obsolescent with the attack on Pearl Harbor by a Japanese strike force with aircraft carriers as the decisive weapon.

The introduction of tanks to the battlefield, necessitated the development of armor-piercing, anti-tank armament. As armor thickness increased along with new alloys that were resistant to penetration, increasingly larger anti-tank guns were developed to defeat it.

Shoulder-fired 20mm cannons gave way to small, wheeled 37mm and 40mm cannons. Tank main guns increased in caliber, muzzle velocity and range, and armor-piercing shells were developed with hardened penetrating cores. High explosive shells with shaped charges such as the American HEAT (High Explosive Anti-Tank) round also appeared and were very effective.

By the latter part of World War II, high velocity tank main guns appeared on the battlefield. The awesome German 88 on the Wehrmacht's Tiger and King Tiger tanks ruled the World War II battlefield, until the arrival of the American M26 Pershing Heavy Tank with its equally deadly 90mm main gun.

Meanwhile lightly armored, but fast tank destroyers relied on speed and maneuver to place high velocity, 76mm armor-piercing rounds into the lighter-armored sides and rear of enemy tanks. The American M18 Hellcat had a top speed of 60 mph (92 kph) making it the fastest tank destroyer on the WWII battlefield.

Twenty-first Century Artillery

Following World War II, artillery has become increasingly sophisticated with rocket-assisted shells, GPS targeting, cluster munitions, and laser-guided projectiles. The caliber of tank main guns has increased to 120mm, and rifling has given way to a smoothbore tube. Despite the lack of rifling, the 120mm main gun is very accurate. It fires a shell that is a radical departure from earlier armor-piercing designs.

APDS

APDS is an acronym for Armor-Piercing, Discarding Sabot. This projectile uses a kinetic energy penetrator fired at 5,000+ fps. The penetrator is made of depleted uranium, which is a very hard metal. After defeating enemy armor, the depleted uranium's incendiary property comes to the fore, setting fire to stored ammunition and anything flammable inside the tank. APDS can defeat the armor of any known adversary likely to appear on the battlefield even at extreme ranges.

Reenactments and Other Shooting Venues

Civilian artillery buffs have a fair number of opportunities to touch off their vintage cannons and feel

▲ Garry James primes his scale model eighteenth-century Napoleon gun for firing.

▲ A scale model Napoleon gun belches fire and smoke as it launches a lead ball projectile.

the sound and fury of a big gun. On numerous occasions throughout America, Revolutionary War and Civil War re-enactors in full period uniform perform precision artillery firing drills in the face of a determined infantry unit in full charge with colors flying.

Of course, during a re-enactment cannons are firing blank charges, but many such events also have direct-fire competition, firing solid shot or other projectiles at targets up to 1,000 yards.

Big Sandy Machine Gun Shoot

Besides reenactments, machine gun and cannon shoots such as the Big Sandy Shoot in Arizona twice a year attract machine gunners and cannoneers from all over the country for a long weekend of day and night live fire complete with pyrotechnic explosions, tracers and concussion waves from the big guns.

I attended a recent Big Sandy Shoot and shared a firing position with Mike Strong who has an original 10-pounder Parrott rifle. My contribution to the firing line was my ArmaLite AR-50L .50 BMG bolt-action on a modified MG42 anti-aircraft tripod–barely significant by comparison.

Like most sizeable artillery pieces, a 10-pounder Parrott rifle is more than a handful to transport and emplace.

A good-sized toy hauler behind a heavy-duty pickup handled transporting the Parrott rifle approximately 240 miles to Big Sandy in a remote part of the Arizona

▼ A bowling ball mortar (left) and anti-tank cannons toe up to the firing line at the Big Sandy Machine Gun Shoot.

▲ Mike Strong loads a wasp-waist, hollow base projectile into the bore of his Parrott rifle.

desert near Wickiup, Arizona. Four young and eager volunteers came along to manhandle the Parrott rifle onto the firing line and act as gun crew.

Loading and firing the Parrott rifle was straightforward, although a few more modern components (such as aluminum foil to contain the pōwder charge) were used. Mike used a solid lead projectile with a wasp waist that flared to a hollow skirt. This skirt would expand to engage the rifling.

The projectile was rammed over a charge of eight ounces of FFG black powder in its aluminum foil package. A full-power service charge would weigh 16 ounces.

A vent pick was inserted into the flash hole to pierce the aluminum foil and expose the powder charge, followed by a friction primer. A long lanyard was attached, and with a sharp pull, the charge ignited, sending the projectile down range.

A few adjustments to the cannon sight, and the Parrott rifle easily lived up to its reputation for accuracy by hitting a derelict washing machine at more than 800 yards as confirmed by a laser rangefinder.

I took a stroll down the quarter-mile long firing line, admiring the vast array of machine guns and cannons of every description. I had hoped to see an acquaintance from Colorado who was a frequent participant at Big Sandy. Lon Laufman had an immaculate M116 75mm pack howitzer, which ranked high on my "gotta have one o' these" list. Unfortunately, he wasn't there. Trekking from northern Colorado all the way to the remote Arizona desert with a cannon in tow is a major undertaking, so I didn't blame him for sitting one out. Still, I was disappointed.

I had visited Lon at his home a few months earlier where he showed me his pack howitzer, but I had looked forward to seeing it in action at Big Sandy. Maybe next time.

▲ An assistant rams a charge into the bore of Mike Strong's Parrott Rifle.

▲ An enormous cloud of smoke erupts as Mike Strong's Parrott rifle sends its projectile downrange at the Big Sandy Machine Gun Shoot.

▲ Mike Strong aims his Parrott rifle.

▼ Lon Laufman, a former artillery instructor at Aberdeen Proving Ground, opens the breech of his M116 75mm pack howitzer.

My trip to Colorado had made me realize what a complex piece of machinery a modern (well sorta modern) artillery piece is. Civil War artillery, such as Mike's Parrott rifle, needs little more than bore cleaning supplies, some axle grease and occasional elbow grease to keep it properly maintained, but modern artillery, even as small as the M116, requires a fair amount of technical knowledge and skill to keep its hydro-pneumatic recoil system, firing mechanism and other complex components properly lubricated and maintained.

Lon, who is a former artillery instructor at Aberdeen Proving Ground, has that kind of knowledge and skill.

I, to my sorrow, do not. Nevertheless, I look forward to the opportunity to pull the lanyard on Lon's pack howitzer at a future Big Sandy Shoot.

On Friday morning at Big Sandy, a buzz of excitement went through the crowd. The Hellcat was here.

The firing line at Big Sandy is on an elevated ridge line that commands a view of the surrounding terrain. Within minutes, spectators had lined the ridge top to watch the drama unfold.

Soon, we could hear the roar of a powerful tank engine accompanied by the unmistakable creak and clank of its treads as a World War II M18 Hellcat tank destroyer hove into view escorted proudly by a

This M18 Hellcat tank destroyer kicks up a cloud of dust as it fires its high velocity 76mm main gun at the Big Sandy Machine Gun Shoot.

▲ An open breech illuminates the rifled bore of an M116 75mm pack howitzer, which can deliver accurate, indirect fire up to five miles away.

World War II jeep armed with a Browning machine gun on a pedestal mount. We watched as the procession made stately progress along the access road to the inclined ramp, then up to the top of the firing line ridge. Onlookers parted to each side watching the powerful armored vehicle rumble down the length of the firing line to take its place near the right end.

Later in the day spectators would be offered an opportunity to fire the Hellcat's powerful 76mm main gun—for a price, which was $230 a pop. Two-and-a-half-foot-long anti-tank ammo ain't cheap!

Did I mention that the Big Sandy Shoot is a heckuva lot a' fun?

The M116 75mm pack howitzer has a horizontal sliding breech, allowing an eight pound projectile with a semi-fixed brass case to be loaded. A base
wder charge with up to three additional powder increments can hurl the projectile to a maximum range of approximately five miles.

Appendix 1. Legally Transferring Class III Firearms and Silencers under the National Firearms Act

enerally speaking, American citizens may own firearms and silencers that fall under the provisions of the National Firearms Act. If you can legally acquire a rifle handgun or shotgun from an FFL (Federal Firearms License) dealer in your state, you are eligible to acquire an NFA weapon—except that many states restrict ownership of some, or all NFA weapons.

Defining a Class III Weapon

There are several general types of NFA weapons, also known as Class III weapons. These are: machine guns (capable of full-auto or burst-fire by a single pull of the trigger); short-barreled rifles (barrel shorter than 16 inches or overall length shorter than 26 inches), short barreled shotguns (barrel shorter than 18 inches or overall length shorter than 26 inches), silencers (device designed to muffle the firing noise of a portable firearm), destructive devices (most firearms with a bore over ½ inch diameter, explosive shells, etc.), and "any other weapon" (AOW) (certain "novelty guns" [such as cane guns and pen guns], smooth bore pistols and various other such devices). More detailed definitions are available on the internet.

By my count, at least twenty-six states and the District of Columbia have restrictions on ownership of NFA firearms and/or silencers. This may range from outright prohibition to merely state licensing and/or registration. Depending on which state, these restrictions might apply to all or only some NFA weapons. For example the state of Washington prohibits machine guns, short barreled rifles and shotguns, etc., but silencers are legal to own.

The lesson here is to *make sure you know and understand your state's laws concerning NFA weapons* before you begin the process of acquisition.

If you decide you want to own a full-automatic weapon, silencer or other NFA weapon, the process is lengthy, invasive to your privacy, and not cheap, but it is far from impossible. For full-auto guns, it has become *outrageously* expensive and prices will continue to climb as time goes on.

McClure-Volkmer Act

The culprit is the McClure-Volkmer Act (also known as the Firearm Owners Protection Act), which was enacted in 1986. This law was generally of benefit to gun owners by ending years of prosecution abuses by the ATF and other government entities, eased ammunition record-keeping and shipment restrictions, and eliminated other onerous obstacles to gun owners. However, an eleventh hour amendment to the House bill was inserted that prohibited civilian ownership of fully-automatic firearms manufactured after May 19, 1986.

This did not prohibit civilian ownership of full-auto weapons manufactured prior to that date, but market forces came into play that drove prices inexorably through the roof. Although many thousands of legally registered full-auto weapons would remain legal to own, this was a fixed number—and consumer demand would rise steadily over the years. The result was a steep inflationary curve with no end in sight.

Outrageous Price Inflation

Today (early 2014), a civilian-legal, basic, semi-auto AR-15 rifle is priced at well under $1,000 retail by numerous manufacturers. On the other hand, a few Vietnam-era select-fire, full-auto M-16s are owned legally by civilians in the United States. The only significant difference between these M-16s and its civilian counterpart (AR-15) is that the M-16 has a select-fire, full-auto capability, and the AR-15 does not.

If you want to buy an M-16 today, expect to fork over upwards of $20,000 for the privilege. That's a twenty-fold increase (or more), but other full-auto firearms may have a price tag even higher. A Thompson, M21 or M28A1 in good condition might set you back $30,000 or more.

This upward spiral applies only to full-auto weapons, not other NFA firearms or silencers. The process to obtain these is still time-consuming, invasive, and it involves a $200 transfer tax on top of the sales price—so it is not cheap. Still, to obtain these items, we don't face the outrageous inflation attached to full-auto firearms.

Four Options

There are several paths you can take to own an NFA weapon or silencer. The least complicated way is to apply as an individual. This requires an FBI background check, complete with fingerprints, photo, etc. and approval by your chief local law enforcement official.

It is also possible to acquire an NFA weapon or silencer through a corporation or through a firearms trust, which bypasses the need for some of the above requirements and has certain other advantages.

A fourth way is to become a federal firearms license holder then pay an annual Class III Special Occupational Tax (Class III license). This, of course, has a number of additional costs and requirements that might not be feasible for you.

For the purposes of this discussion, let's set aside the corporation and FFI options because they both have far-reaching consequences that include additional IRS scrutiny, rigorous record-keeping, 24/7 access to business premises, and other onerous legal requirements.

These two avenues shouldn't be entered into lightly, certainly not for something as simple as acquiring an NFA weapon. That leaves individual acquisition or creating a firearms trust as the best avenues for acquiring an NFA firearm or silencer.

Individual Acquisition

Any individual who wishes to acquire an NFA firearm or silencer must be twenty-one and must not be otherwise prohibited from possessing or owning a firearm. If you qualify, you should check the state laws of your home state to ensure that you may legally own an NFA firearm/silencer and comply with your state's legal requirements (if any).

If these requirements are met, you must complete (in duplicate) an ATF Form 4 Application for Tax Paid Transfer and Registration of Firearm. Two recent passport-type photos of the transferee and two properly completed FBI Forms FD-258 (fingerprint cards) must be attached to the ATF Form 4. Signatures on both copies must be original and in ink.

Before sending the application to the Bureau of Alcohol, Tobacco, Firearms and Explosives (BATFE), it must be submitted to your local Chief Law Enforcement Officer (CLEO). This normally means the Chief of Police in your city or town of residence, the sheriff of your county of residence, the head of the State Police in your state of residence, or the District Attorney having jurisdiction in your area. The CLEO will fill out the appropriate section of the back of the Form 4, certifying that he has no information that the receipt or possession of the NFA firearm/silencer would place the transferee in violation of state law.

Note: *Some CLEOs may decline to provide such certification, and this will often derail your transfer.*

When the CLEO returns the certified Form 4s you must submit both copies to the National Firearms Act Branch of the BATFE along with a check or money order for $200 payable to the BATFE. (If your state requires any permits in connection with the transaction, include this, too.) You will undergo a background check and— barring mistakes in your application—you should receive your approved Form 4 with a $200 tax stamp affixed to certify payment.

Only after receiving the approved Form 4 can you legally take possession of your NFA firearm or silencer. When you take possession, you will complete a Form 4473 as you would for a normal purchase of a firearm from an FFL dealer. However, no NCIS background check is not necessary since that was completed upon submitting the Form 4.

All transfers of NFA devices must go through a Class III dealer in your state—except that you may legally transfer a second-hand NFA firearm/silencer from a legal owner **in your state of residence**. Having said that, I recommend that **without exception** you funnel all such transactions through a local Class III dealer.

A local Class III dealer can guide you through the whole process, keep you compliant with any and all state and local laws, and help you avoid pitfalls along the way. Any fee he charges will be well worth it in expediting your application and saving you associated aggravation.

Negative Issues

First, the federal background check is a serious intrusion into your personal privacy. As an NFA applicant, you have no way to get around this issue. This might not bother you, but if it does, you just have to accept it. In addition you need to be aware of a few obligations you might not have thought about in connection with your NFA firearms/silencers.

Second: You may not loan your NFA firearm/silencer to anyone, nor can you store it at a friend's house unless it is locked away so only you have access to it. A gray area exists about whether you may even allow someone else to handle or shoot it in your presence.

Third: If you wish to travel to another state with your NFA firearm or silencer, you must request permission from the BATFE by letter or on an ATF Form 5320.20. If you choose the letter option, it must include your (registrant's) name; which NFA firearm/silencer(s); current location of the firearms(s); location where the items will be transported; dates and means of travel; reason for travel; whether move is temporary or permanent; whether movement will involve transfer of ownership; and whether possession of the weapon will violate local or state law at your destination. The Form 5320.20 covers all these questions. If the travel will violate the law, BATFE will deny permission.

Fourth: If you move your residence, you are required to notify BATFE of your change of address.

Fifth: Even though you are the legal owner of an NFA firearm/silencer, state or local law may prohibit you from using it for hunting and/or target practice.

NFA Firearms Trust Acquisition

A lesser known, but attractive alternative to individual acquisition of an NFA firearm/silencer is an NFA Firearms Trust. The legal definition of a trust is: A fiduciary relationship in which one party, known as a trustor, gives another party, the trustee, the right to hold title to property or assets for the benefit of a third party, the beneficiary.

Attributes and Caveats

An NFA Firearms Trust, if drafted properly by an attorney who understands NFA legal issues, is devoted solely to hold firearms, ammunition and firearms-related accessories, such as riflescopes. It should **NOT** cover other property, such as real estate, jewelry, etc. You should be aware that some attorneys, operating outside their main area of expertise, might try to modify a standard living trust to cover firearms. This can create problems down the line, including instructing a trustee to do something that is illegal under the NFA statutes and regulations.

Benefits of an NFA Firearms Trust

Right from the get-go, transferring an NFA firearm or silencer to a trust instead of an individual simplifies and streamlines the process. Because the transfer is to the trust instead of an individual, no CLEO approval is needed. Neither do you need to provide fingerprint cards or photos.

Unlike an individual transfer, NFA firearms/silencers belonging to a trust may be used or possessed by any person designated as a trustee. Also, when the trustor (you) dies, the firearms in the trust (and associated property) passes to the designated beneficiary without paying the $200 transfer tax or becoming entangled in probate. This process involves a number of steps to comply with the law, but they are spelled out in the trust documents.

Note: The Obama Administration and the BATFE are in the process of proposing rule changes that will affect gun trusts, so keep up to date on this. If you decide to create an NFA Gun Trust, sooner is better than later.

Restating a Caveat

Drafting a valid, airtight NFA gun trust is a job for a highly qualified attorney, and will cost a few hundred dollars to complete. Do your homework and satisfy yourself that your NFA gun trust is a valid document, not a repurposed general living trust. A great deal of information is available on the internet. One website that I regard highly is *www.guntrustlawyer.com*. However, there are numerous other sites, including Wikipedia, where you can obtain information.

Enjoy!

Despite all the complications and hoops you must jump through, owning and shooting a full-auto and/or silenced firearm is what is commonly called ". . . a real HOOT!" I personally believe it is well worth the aggravation, time, and expense. I hope you do too.

AZ1 8604

OMB No 1140-0014 (11/30/2010)

U.S. Department of Justice
Bureau of Alcohol, Tobacco, Firearms and Explosives

Application for Tax Paid Transfer and Registration of Firearm

ATF Control Number	Submit in Duplicate to: National Firearms Act Branch

2a. Transferee's Name and Address *(Including tradename, if any) (See instruction 2)*

Stanley Jerome Skinner

2b. County

3a. Transferor's Name and Address *(Including trade name, if any) (Executors: see instruction 2k)*

Alton Michael Strong
Pima Technologies

3b. Transferor's Telephone Number and Area Code

3c. If Applicable: Decedent's Name, Address, and Date of Death

co, Firearms
530298

W300-358
AF

ation a check or
ropriate amount
eau of Alcohol,
xplosives. Upon
on, this office
ncel the required
stamp for you
and 3.)

3d. Number, Street, City, State and Zip Code of Residence *(or Firearms Business Premises)* if Different from Item 3a.

The above-named and undersigned transferor hereby makes application as required by Section 5812 of the National Firearms Act to transfer and register the firearm described below to the transferee

4 Description of Firearm *(Complete items a through h)*

a. Name and Address of Manufacturer and/or Importer of Firearm	b. Type of Firearm *(See instruction 1c)*	c Caliber, Gauge or Size *(Specify)*	d. Model		
SSK Industries **590 Woodvue Lane** **Wintersville, OH 43952**			N/A		
			Length *(Inches)*	e. Of Barrel: N/A	f. Overall: 12"
	Silencer	.30	g Serial Number W300-358		

h. Additional Description or Data Appearing on Firearm *(Attach additional sheet if necessary)*

5 Transferee's Federal Firearms License *(If any)*				6 Transferee's Special (Occupational) Tax Status *(If any)*	
(Give complete 15-digit number) (See instruction 2b)				a Employer Identification Number	b Class
First 6 digits	2 digits	2 digits	5 digits		

7 Transferor's Federal Firearms License *(If any)*				8 Transferor's Special (Occupational) Tax Status *(If any)*	
(Give complete 15-digit number) (See instruction 2b)				a Employer Identification Number	b Class
First 6 digits	2 digits	2 digits	5 digits		
936019	07	4B	00499	71-0887825	2 Mfg

Under Penalties of Perjury, I Declare that I have examined this application, and to the best of my knowledge and belief it is true, correct and complete, and that the transfer of the described firearm to the transferee and receipt and possession of it by the transferee are not prohibited by the provisions of Chapter 44, Title 18, United States Code; Chapter 53, Title 26, United States Code; or Title VII of the Omnibus Crime Control and Safe Streets Act, as amended, or any provisions of State or local law

9 Consent to Disclosure of Information to Transferee *(See instruction 8)* I **Do** or **Do Not** *(Circle one)* Authorize ATF to Provide Information Relating to this Application to the Above-Named Transferee.

10 Signature of Transferor *(or authorized official)*	11 Name and Title of Authorized Official *(Print or type)* Alton Michael Strong, Owner	12. Date FEB 7, 2011

The Space Below is for the use of the Bureau of Alcohol, Tobacco, Firearms and Explosives

By authority of the Director, This Application has been Examined, and the Transfer and Registration of the Firearm Described herein and the Interstate Movement of that Firearm, when Applicable, to the Transferee are

Stamp Denomination
200

☐ Approved *(with the following conditions, if any)*

☐ Disapproved *(For the following reasons)*

Signature of Authorized ATF Official

Date DEC 1 5 2011

ATF Form 4 (5320.4)
Revised March 2006

▲ The front side of an actual approved BATFE Form 4 shows the $200 tax stamp affixed as proof of payment for a silencer transfer.

Transferee Information

The following questions must be answered by any transferee who is **not** a Federal firearms licensee or government agency. The transferee shall give full details on a separate sheet for all "YES" answers. *(See instruction 2d)*

13. Are You:	Yes	No	14. Have You:	Yes	No
a. Charged by information or under indictment in any court for a crime punishable by imprisonment for a term exceeding one year?	☐	☒	a. Been convicted in any court of a crime for which the judge could have imprisoned you for more than one year, even if the judge actually gave you a shorter sentence?	☐	☒
b. A **fugitive** from justice?	☐	☒	b. Been discharged from the armed forces under **dishonorable** conditions?	☐	☒
c. An alien who is **illegally** or unlawfully in the United States?	☐	☒	c. Been adjudicated mentally defective or been committed to a mental institution?	☐	☒
d. Under 21 years of age?	☐	☒	d. Renounced your United States citizenship?	☐	☒
e. An unlawful user of or addicted to, marijuana, or any depressant, stimulant, or narcotic drug, or any other controlled substance?	☐	☒	e. Been convicted in any court of a misdemeanor crime of domestic violence? This includes any misdemeanor conviction involving the use or attempted use of physical force committed by a current or former spouse, parent, or guardian of the victim, or by a person with a similar relationship with the victim.	☐	☒
f. Subject to a court order restraining you from harassing, stalking or threatening an intimate partner or child of such partner?	☐	☒			

15. Transferee's Certification *(See instruction 2e)*

I, ___Stanley Jerome Skinner___ , have a reasonable necessity to
(Name of Transferee)

possess the machinegun, short-barreled rifle, short-barreled shotgun, or destructive device described on this application for the following reason(s) _____

___to enhance my personal collection___

and my possession of the device or weapon would be consistent with public safety (18 U.S.C. 922(b) (4) and 27 CFR 478.98).

UNDER PENALTIES OF PERJURY, I declare that I have examined this application and the documents submitted in support thereof, and to the best of my knowledge and belief it is true, correct and complete.

___(Signature of Transferee)___   ___4/20/11___
(Signature of Transferee)   *(Date)*

17. Law Enforcement Certification *(See instruction 2e)*

I certify that I am the chief law enforcement officer of the organization named below having jurisdiction in the area of residence of

___Stanley Jerome Skinner___   I have no information indicating that the transferee will use the firearm or device
(Name of Transferee)

described on this application for other than lawful purposes. I have no information that the receipt or possession of the firearm or device described in item 4 would be place the transferee in violation of State or local law.

___Sheriff C. Dupnik___   ___May 9, 2011___
(Signature and Title of Chief Law Enforcement Officer)   *(Date)*

___Pima County Sheriff's Department 1750 E. Benson Highway, Tucson, AZ 85714___
(Organization and Street Address)

___Pima___   ___(520) 351-4600___
(County)   *(Telephone Number)*

Important Information for Currently Registered Firearms

If this registration document evidences the current registration of the firearm described on it, please note the following information.

Estate Procedures: For procedures regarding the transfer of firearms in an estate resulting from the death of the registrant identified in item 2a, the executor should contact the NFA Branch, Bureau of Alcohol, Tobacco, Firearms and Explosives, 244 Needy Road, Martinsburg, WV 25405.

Change of Address: Unless currently licensed under the Gun Control Act, the registrant shall notify the NFA Branch, Bureau of Alcohol, Tobacco, Firearms and Explosives, 244 Needy Road, Martinsburg, WV 25405, in writing, of any change to the address in Item 2a.

Change of Description: The registrant shall notify the NFA Branch, Bureau of Alcohol, Tobacco, Firearms and Explosives, 244 Needy Road, Martinsburg, WV 25405, in writing, of any change to the description of the firearm in Item 4.

Interstate Movement: If the firearm identified in item 4 is a machinegun, short-barreled rifle, short-barreled shotgun, or destructive device, the registrant may be required by 18 U.S.C. § 922(a)(4) to obtain permission from ATF prior to any transportation in interstate or foreign commerce.

Restrictions on Possession: Any restriction *(see approval block on face of form)* on the possession of the firearm identified in item 4 continues with the further transfer of the firearm.

Persons Prohibited from Possessing Firearms: If the registrant becomes prohibited by 18 U.S.C. § 922 from possessing a firearm, the registrant shall notify the NFA Branch, Bureau of Alcohol, Tobacco, Firearms and Explosives, 244 Needy Road, Martinsburg, WV 25405, in writing, immediately upon becoming prohibited for guidance on the disposal of the firearm.

Proof of Registration: This approved application is the registrant's proof of registration and it shall be made available to any ATF officer upon request.

ATF Form 4 (5320.4)
Revised March 2006

▲ The reverse side of an actual approved BATFE Form 4 shows the passport-sized photo of the transferee affixed to the document. It also shows the CLEO certification by the County Sheriff.

Appendix 2. Assembling an AR-15 Lower Receiver

he M16, in its current variations, is now entering its sixth decade of service with all branches of American military forces. Despite its longevity, the M16 and its civilian cousin, the AR-15, was not always popular among civilian shooters.

A reputation for mediocre accuracy ensured that interest in the AR-15 was, at best, tepid. But as light-recoiling National Match-grade AR-15s began winning service rifle long-range matches, the public's attitude slowly changed. By the late 1980s, advent of "flat-top" versions of the AR-15 had begun to transform the staid AR-15A2 into something completely different.

Unlike its service rifle predecessors, the AR-15 boasted "modular construction," meaning that component groups, such as the buttstock, upper and lower receiver groups, pistol grips, etc. could have different configurations and could be easily swapped-out, which opened seemingly endless possibilities for an individual to customize his AR-15 according to his personal preferences.

Then came the 1994 federal law banning so-called assault rifles and high-capacity magazines. Suddenly public interest in the AR-15 and its Soviet counterpart, the AK47 peaked. The law did not apply to firearms manufactured before the law's enactment, so "grandfathered" pre-ban AR-15s with flash hiders, folding stocks, pistol grips and the dreaded high-capacity magazines brought premium prices at gun shows and dealerships across the nation.

American Ingenuity

When the 1994 law expired under its "sunset" clause a cottage industry developed to meet a sudden demand for AR-15 components and accessories. In previous generations, young Americans had built street hot-rods, assembled powerful "audiophile" stereo systems and cobbled together innovative personal computers and software that humbled proud corporations such as IBM.

Now the same thing was happening to the AR-15 with its modular construction. If you wanted a flat-top AR-15 with a 16-inch barrel, quad-rail forend, six-position folding stock—no problem. How about a 20-inch barrel

chambered for .450 Beowulf, .458 SOCOM or even a suppressed, ultra-quiet .300 Whisper? No problem.

The possibilities are limited only by the shooter's imagination.

Now you didn't even have to begin with a complete weapon. Now manufacturers offered custom upper receiver assemblies in many variations. All you had to do was pop two take-down pins, remove the old upper assembly and replace it with the new one.

The same thing is true of the lower receiver assembly. If you want a fixed butt stock, fine—or maybe a GI mil-spec folding stock, equally okay. How about an ergonomic pistol grip or match-grade trigger assembly? You got it.

Do It Yourself

This brings us to assembling a complete lower receiver group from a stripped lower receiver. Precision CNC machining has made it possible to manufacture a high-quality stripped lower receiver that can sell as cheaply as $60-$70 retail. It is also possible to spend upwards of $200 on a stripped receiver if you simply must have a prestigious brand name on it, but trust me, the $60–$70 receiver is every bit as good.

Incidentally, the BATFE considers the AR-15 lower receiver to be a firearm. It must have a serial number, and your friendly FFI dealer will give you a Form 4473 to fill out and make the obligatory NCIS phone call before you complete the transaction and take it home with you.

I find it interesting (but logical, I suppose) that a complete AR-15 *upper* receiver assembly with bolt carrier group, fully chambered barrel, and foreend is **NOT** a firearm. You may buy it online and have it shipped directly to your home.

But I digress.

The subject here is the AR-15 stripped lower receiver and how to assemble the necessary component parts to make it a fully functioning lower receiver group.

Necessary Components

Obviously, you will need a lower receiver parts kit, which is available from internet sources such as Brownell's or Midway. This includes all small parts and springs for the hammer and trigger assembly,

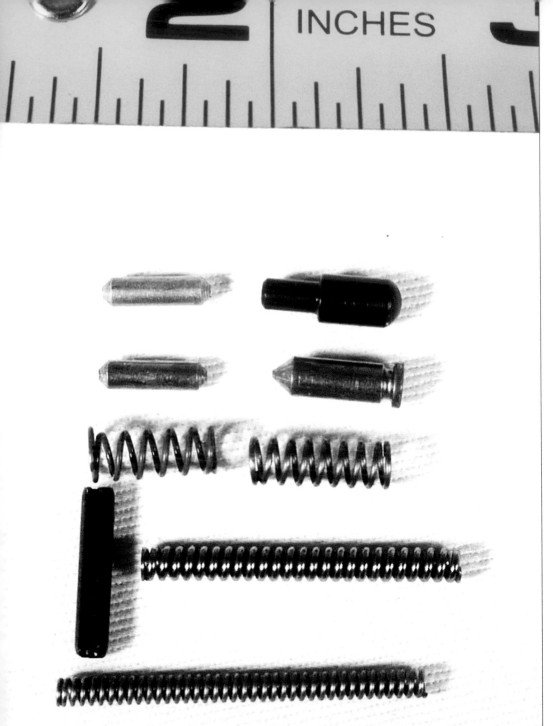

◄ An AR-15 lower receiver parts kit contains numerous small springs and parts. Some of them are as small as a grain of rice.

safety latch, take-down pins, magazine release and pistol grip.

The other necessary item is a buttstock assembly. This is also available from numerous sources on the Internet. Like other custom choices you can make this can be a relatively inexpensive telescoping buttstock, a fixed A2-style stock or any of a number of custom butt stock assemblies. You can find butt stocks designed to give you quicker sight alignment, a more rigid shooting platform or other features that manufacturers hope will persuade you to pay $200 or more for their product.

Personally, I am satisfied with a simple mil spec telescoping butt stock, but you might feel differently.

Necessary Instructions, Tools, etc.

Assembling an AR-15 lower receiver is well within the capability of anyone who has some degree of experience with hand tools—and who is capable

A detailed assembly guide such as this guide by Walt Kuleck and Clint McKee offers valuable assembly instructions and helps you avoid pitfalls that can ruin your project.

of understanding detailed instructions. It's a project that can be completed in an afternoon, but you need to understand that it is not a walk in the park. Numerous pitfalls in the process can cause you serious heartburn or ruin your project.

For this reason, you need detailed assembly instructions such as *The AR-15 Complete Assembly Guide* by Walt Kuleck with Clint McKee. With this in hand, you must make sure you understand each step and

proceed with care. Do this and you can take a degree of pride in your new AR-15 that you'd never have with a store-bought firearm. You will also gain a fine understanding of how your AR-15's internal parts work, which is both useful and satisfying.

Your parts kit contains several parts ranging from small to tiny. Among them are a pivot pin detent and a takedown detent that are about the size of a grain of rice. These and other parts are spring-loaded and

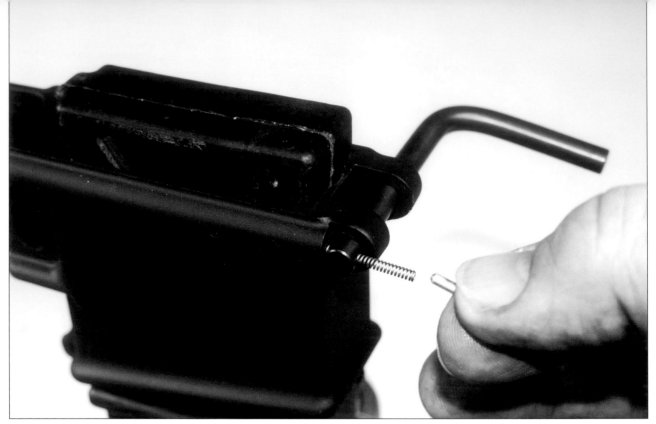

▲ The pivot pin installation tool is a simple L-shaped rod with a hole in the end. This tool allows you to compress the pivot pin detent spring and detent into its recess. Then you rotate it 90 degrees to hold the detent and spring in place while you slide the pivot pin in place. The detent engages a groove in the pivot pin that holds the pin captive.

▲ One of the essential tools is an AR collapsible stock wrench, which engages a castellated nut that holds the buffer tube and back plate snug against the rear of the lower receiver.

a small slip can launch them with considerable force into parts unknown—or into your eye with a result you won't like. **For this reason safety glasses are essential.** Wear them at all times as you work on this project.

Several common tools such as a small gunsmith's hammer or mallet and screwdriver set are necessary to assemble an AR-15 lower receiver. Also, you should have certain specialized tools on hand. Some of them are absolutely essential. Others will make your project an enjoyable experience rather than an afternoon of endless frustration or misery.

Among the specialized tools is a pivot pin installation tool. This is a deceptively simple L-shaped steel rod with a small hole near one end. With it, installing a pivot pin with its spring-loaded detent is an easy task that takes less than a minute. Without it, you will launch several aforementioned rice-grain-sized detents into the far corners of your work area, never to be found. Incidentally, Brownell's and Midway will cheerfully sell you spares.

You will also need a magazine well vise block; a butt stock spanner wrench; a set of roll pin starter punches; a set of roll pin punches and a set of plain punches. All of these items are available from Brownell's or Midway.

Is it Worth it?

By now, you probably think this is a lot of trouble to go to just to assemble something you can buy already complete. This includes the need to buy several tools that have little use except for assembling an AR-15 lower receiver. Trust me on this, these tools involve only a modest cash investment, and you will probably discover (as I did) that this is not a one-time project. The enjoyment you get will make you want to do it again and again.

I have assembled five lowers and have another sitting on my bench ready to go. I haven't tried to assemble an upper receiver and barrel group yet, but I suspect it is only a matter of time before I tackle that task, too.

So, take the plunge, you'll be glad you did.

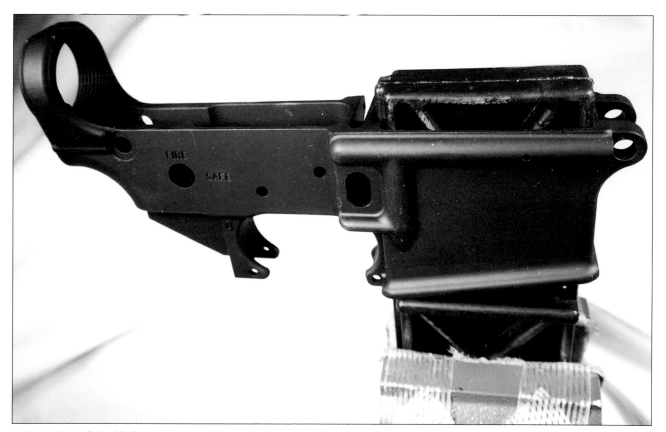

▲ A magazine well vise block inserts into the lower receiver magazine well to hold the receiver firmly during the assembly process.

Glossary

Active NVD: night vision devices that produce their own form of illumination only detectable by a specially designed optical receiver, thereby providing the user with improved visibility in low light conditions

APDS: armor-piercing discarding sabot, a kind of round used primarily for anti-tank purposes

AK: *Avtomat Kalashnikova*, Russian for "automatic Kalashnikov"

AKM: a modernized version of the classic AK assault rifle

AOW: "any other weapon", a classification laid out in the National Firearms Act that includes novelty firearms, cane and pen guns, and smooth bore pistols

BAR: Browning Automatic Rifle

Barrel clamp: an attachment placed on the barrel of a firearm that allows for accessorizing of the weapon (e.g. weapon slings, tactical lights, etc.)

BATFE: Bureau of Alcohol, Tobacco, Firearms, and Explosives

Blowback action: a firing mechanism where the rearward movement of a cartridge, in response to ignited propellant, provides the energy that ejects the spent cartridge and chambers a new round

Boat tail: the slight inward tapering at the base of supersonic bullets, incorporated to reduce air resistance while in flight

Bolt-action: an operating system where the cartridge is manually inserted and extracted from the chamber by operating a bolt on the side of the firearm

Bore: see "Gauge"

Boxlock action: a firing mechanism in break-open rifles and shotguns where the hammer is encased in the receiver

BPE: black powder express, a form of round common before the introduction of the nitro express round

Break-open: a type of firearm that breaks open where the base of the barrel meets the receiver, allowing the shooter to insert and extract rounds

Breechloader: a type of firearm that has a breech in the receiver through which the shooter inserts rounds

BMG: Browning Machine Gun

Buffer: a component of a full-automatic or semi-automatic rifle that uses a spring or cushioning material to absorb recoil force, which reduces stress on internal action parts. On a full-automatic rifle it also helps regulate rate of fire.

Buffer tube: a component of the AR-15/M16 receiver that helps both in returning the bolt to its original position (thereby chambering another round) and in reducing the recoil passed to the shooter, commonly by the use of a spring that absorbs the force of the recoil. The absorption of the recoil also helps reduce stress on internal parts of the rifle.

Bull barrel: a barrel type that is equally cylindrical from the breech to the muzzle, thereby reducing aim-affecting vibrations at the expense of increased weight

Carbine: a conversion of a rifle where it is reduced in size and weight while still maintaining its firing power and characteristics. Typically used by military personnel in roles necessitating high-mobility.

Centerfire cartridge: a type of round that has a primer centered at its base and which is ignited by the striking of a firearm's hammer or pin

Chamber pressure: the pressure exerted by the cartridge shell on the chamber of a firearm when its propellant is ignited, typically expressed as PSI or CUP

CIP: *Commission Internationale Permanente pour l'Épreuve des Armes à Feu Portatives*, the Permanent International Commission for Firearms Testing, a multinational European organization primarily concerned with the testing of firearm rounds

CLEO: Chief Law Enforcement Officer

Closed bolt: in semi- and full-automatic rifles, a firing mechanism that involves the bolt remaining closed up until, and after, the firing and ejection of a round

Cocking lever: a component of a firearm that brings back the hammer and allows for the moving of the bolt

Cooling fins: an barrel attachment that helps dissipate the heat generated by an ignited round

Cordite: a smokeless propellant which was used in cartridges, at the time being an improvement over black powder

Coriolis effect: the effect exerted on a bullet's in-flight trajectory by the movement of the Earth's rotation

CQB: close quarters combat

CUP: copper units of pressure, used to measure the chamber pressure in firearms

Delta ring: a component of a firearm that joins the fore end to the receiver

Destructive device: a term used by the ATF to denote any high-powered armament

Direct impingement operating system: a firing mechanism that channels excess gas from a fired round directly back to the receiver to effect the chambering of a new round

Double base propellant: see "Cordite"

Double-action: a firing mechanism where a single trigger pull both cocks and releases a firearm's hammer

Express cartridges: A term coined in the 1850s by James Purdey to denote a round that traveled at a higher-than-normal velocity. The term is today primarily used to denote large-bore rounds for hunting large or dangerous game.

FFL: Federal Firearms License

Fixed firing pin: in rifles, a small projection on the bolt that strikes and ignites a chambered round

Fixed Trigger: a trigger that is exposed whether the hammer or striker is cocked or uncocked and is commonly protected by a trigger guard. This is unlike a folding trigger, which is exposed only when the hammer is cocked. Otherwise a folding trigger is hidden, usually in the pistol grip or butt stock.

Flatshooter: a cartridge with a high muzzle velocity loaded using a pointed bullet with a high ballistic coefficient, which results in a relatively shallow trajectory. Also, a rifle chambered for such a cartridge.FLIR: forward looking infrared

Floating firing pin: a component of a firearm used to strike and ignite a chambered round and that sits freely in the receiver or the bolt

Fluting: the removal of material from the exterior of a barrel or bolt in order to reduce weight, typically in the form of lengthwise grooves

FPS: feet per second

Gas-operated action: a firing mechanism that uses the expanding gas from an ignited propellant to eject the expended cartridge and chamber a new one

Gauge: also called "bore," a unit of measurement based on the weight of a solid sphere of lead and used for measuring the diameter of a firearm's barrel

Grain: a unit of measurement for bullets and propellants

Crossbolt: in break-open rifles and shotguns, a bolt that serves to lock the barrel and receiver together

Hammer spur: the portion of a hammer that allows for manual operation

Hammer: the component of a firearm that strikes a chambered round and ignites the propellant

Hand-finds-hand: a firing technique where the shooter can reload without moving their eyes from their target

HEAT: high explosive anti-tank

Hydro-pneumatic recoil mechanism: a means of reducing recoil in artillery by using compressed air and hydraulic oil to slowly dissipate the barrel's energy

Ma deuce: unofficial name for the Browning .50 caliber machine gun

MG: *Maschinengewehr*, German for "machine gun"

MP: *Maschinenpistole*, German for "machine pistol"

MOA: minute of arc/angle, a unit used by shooters to compensate for bullet drop over long distances

Muzzle brake: a component of a firearm, generally at the end of the barrel, which redirects gas to compensate for recoil

Muzzle flip: the kicking motion a barrel makes when a firearm is being fired

Muzzle velocity: the speed a bullet has the moment it leaves the end of a firearm's barrel

Muzzleloader: a type of firearm that requires the round be loaded through the muzzle of the barrel

NE: nitro express, a kind of high-velocity round that replaced the black powder express round

NFA: National Firearms Act

NVD: night vision device

Open-bolt: in semi- and full-automatic rifles, a firing mechanism that involves the bolt remaining open up until, and after, the firing and ejection of a round

Operating pressure: the force required to affect the firing and chambering mechanisms of a firearm

Over/under rifles: a firearm design that places two barrels vertically, one on top of the other

Passive NVD: night vision devices that augment ambient light to provide a user with improved visibility in low light conditions

Picatinny rail: a grooved sleeve placed over the barrel of certain firearms and on which can be affixed various attachments (e.g. scopes, lasers, tactical lights, grenade launcher)

Primer: the component of a cartridge that is struck to ignite the propellant and shoot the bullet

Plinking: a form of shooting practice that involves firing at small metallic targets

Push-feed action: a chambering mechanism where the bolt of a firearm simply pushes a round in the chamber, rather than clamping on to the rim of the round

Rebated boat tail: the slight "step" at the base of supersonic bullets, incorporated to reduce air resistance while in flight

Receiver: the component of a firearm that contains all of its moving parts

Recoil-operated action: a mechanism that uses the recoil of a fired round to affect the chambering of a new round

Rifled: the spiraling grooves inside of a barrel that make a fire bullet spin in flight, giving it a more consistent trajectory

Rimfire cartridge: a type of round that is ignited by a firearm's hammer or pin striking it at its base

Rimless cartridge: a type of round on which the rim at the base of the cartridge does not extend beyond the overall width of the round

Rotating bolt: a mechanism that locks a bolt in to place until released

RPK: *Ruchnoy Pulemyot Kalashnikova*, Kalashnikov hand-held machine gun

RPM: rounds per minute

Side-by-side rifle: a firearm design that places two barrels horizontally, one beside the other

Single-action: a firing mechanism where a single trigger pull only releases a firearm's hammer

Starlight scope: a Vietnam War era night vision device that used ambient light provide the user with increased low light visibility

Tang safety: a safety switch on the back of a firearm's stock that can be easily manipulated with the thumb

Telescoping bolt: a kind of bolt that shrouds a portion of the barrel and allows for a more compact firearm

Underlug: a component of a firearm, typically on revolvers, that shrouds the ejector rod and adds weight for increased accuracy

Wildcat cartridge: a cartridge for which firearms and bullets are not mass produced, therefore primarily being the purview of hobbyists

Index

B

H

Hand Cannons. *see also* Smith & Wesson
    .38 Special, 21–22
    .38-44 High Velocity cartridge, 21–22
    .44 Remington Magnum, 22, *23*
    .50 Alaskan (wildcat cartridge), 25, 27
    .375 JDJ cartridge, 25
    .454 Casull, 23–24, 27, *28*
    .458 Winchester Magnum, 25, 27
    .620 JDJ, 25, 27
    Colt Walker revolver, 17–18, *28*
    and "Dirty Harry," 17, 22–23, 27
    Howdah Pistol, 19–21
    most powerful, 23–24, 27
    Ruger Blackhawk .44 Magnum, 22
    Thompson/Center Contender pistol, 24–25
    Thompson/Center Encore, *24*, 25, 27
Handbook of the German Army, 97
handloading data, 69, 71
Harrison, Craig, 83
Hartung, Tyler, *38*, *47*, *60*, *86*
Hathcock, Carlos N., II, 79, 83
HEAT (High Explosive Anti-Tank), 115
Heckler & Koch MP5, 43
Hellcat (M18), 115, *121–122*
Holland & Holland rifles
    .375 H&H Magnum, 6, 7, *8*, 28
    .600 Nitro Express, 9
    commission for wealthy client, 2–4
    H&H Royal Ejector Model (500/465 NE), 7
Hornady ammunition, 28, 31, 68, 69, 75
Howdah Pistol, 19–21
howdahs, 18, 19
howitzers, 109–110, 118, *120*, 121, *122*
hunting
    Bengal tigers, in 19th C. India, 19–21
    dangerous game rifles (DGRs). *see* Express Rifles
    feral hogs. *see* feral hog hunting
    hand cannons
        .460 S&W Magnum revolver, *26*, *28*, *29*, *30*, 31
        .500 S&W Magnum, 28–29, 31
        Howdah Pistol, 19–21
        Thompson/Center Contender pistol, 24–25
    ivory hunting, 1, 2, 16
    varmint, 55, 57, 59, 66, 71–72
hydro-pneumatic recoil system, 110, 113, 121, 136

I

indirect fire, artillery, 111, 113
individual acquisition, of Class III weapons, 125–126
Interarms, 101
International Military Antiques, 101

J

James, Charles T., 110
James, Garry, *19*, *20*, 21, *53*, *63*, 101, *102*, *103*, *116*
James Purdey & Sons, *9*
James rifle, 110
John Rigby & Co., 8
Johnson, Harold, 27
Jones, J. D., 24–25, 27, 68, 94
Jurras, Lee, 24

K

Kalashnikov, Mikhail, 53–54
Kalashnikov AK-47, *53–54*
Keith, Elmer, 21–22
Knob Creek, 95, *96*
Korean War, 39, *41*, 64
Krieghoff Classic Safari, *4*, 10, 11, 12–13
Kurz, German MP-44, *53–54*

L

Lakeside Machine LLC, *51*, 52
Lancaster (gunmaker), 20
Langdon, Jesse D., 99
Laufman, Lon, *35*, 118, *120*, 121
"Leopard Rifle," 9
Leupoid VX3 6.5-20X50 LR scope, *85*
Lewis, Isaac Newton, 93–94
Lewis Gun, 93–94
Linebaugh, John, 27

M

M1 Abrams tank, 95
M-1 Garand service rifle, 34, 54
M3/M3A1 Grease Gun, 39, *41*, 42
M4 Sherman tank, 95
M-16. *see* AR-15

Wolseley, Garnet, 87
World War I
    Lewis Gun, 93–94
    machine gun casualties, 90
    trench warfare, and German MP18/I, 32, 37
World War II
    World War II, and German MP40, 32, *35*

World War II, and Tommy Gun production,
    34–35
WWII, German MG 42, 96–97

X

XM-16E1 (AR-15 variant), 55

Notes

Notes

Notes

Notes

Notes

Notes

Shooter's Bible, 106th Edition

The World's Bestselling Fircarms Reference

Edited by Jay Cassell

Published annually for nearly one hundred years, the *Shooter's Bible* is the most comprehensive and sought-after reference guide for new fircarms and their specifications, as well as for thousands of guns that have been in production and are currently on the market. Nearly every firearms manufacturer in the world is included in this renowned compendium. The 106th edition also contains new and existing product sections on ammunition, optics, and accessories, plus newly updated handgun and rifle ballistic tables along with extensive charts of currently available bullets and projectiles for handloading.

With a timely feature on the newest products on the market, and complete with color and black-and-white photographs featuring various makes and models of firearms and equipment, the *Shooter's Bible* is an essential authority for any beginner or experienced hunter, firearm collector, or gun enthusiast.

$29.95 Paperback • ISBN 978-1-62914-559-4

Shooter's Bible Guide to AR-15s
A Comprehensive Reference to One of America's Favorite Rifles
by Doug Howlett

There's no denying the popularity and intense fascination with AR-15s among firearms enthusiasts today. Here, inside the most comprehensive source to date, is Doug Howlett's expert approach to everything from the intriguing history of the AR to breaking down the weapon piece by piece, choosing ammunition, and even building your own gun.

In this complete book of AR-style firearms, you can peruse the products of all manufacturers, learn about the evolution of the AR from its uses in the military in the 1960s to its adaptation for law enforcement and civilian uses, and gain essential knowledge on the parts and functions of the rifle. Also included are chapters on customizing and accessorizing ARs, with special focus on small gun shops and makers and their unique and successful products. Look into the future of the AR straight from top gun authorities!

$19.95 Paperback • ISBN 978-1-61608-444-8

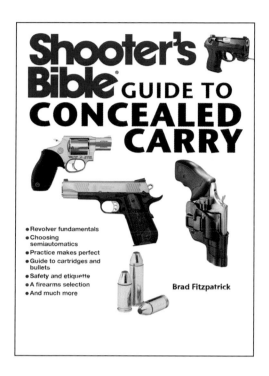

Shooter's Bible Guide to Concealed Carry

by Brad Fitzpatrick

Don't wait to be placed in a dangerous setting faced with an armed attacker. The *Shooter's Bible Guide to Concealed Carry* is an all-encompassing resource that not only offers vital gun terminology but also suggests which gun is the right fit for you and how to efficiently use the device properly, be it in public or at home. Firearm expert Brad Fitzpatrick examines how to practice, how to correct mistakes, and how to safely challenge yourself when you have achieved basic skills. Included within is a comprehensive chart describing the various calibers for concealed carry, suitable instructions for maintaining it, and, most importantly, expert step-by-step instructions for shooting.

$19.95 Paperback • ISBN 978-1-62087-580-3

Shooter's Bible Guide to Home Defense
A Comprehensive Handbook on How to Protect Your Property from Intrusion and Invasion
by Roger Eckstine

Do you feel vulnerable in your own home? The *Shooter's Bible Guide to Home Defense* was written to help you trade in your fears for a feeling of vigilance, readiness, and pride. This is not a catalog of gimmicks, gadgets, and drills that only a Navy SEAL can perform but an intense look at how to fortify your home discreetly and protect yourself from home invaders. Learn how to choose weapons and use them under stress. Gain legal perspective, sharpen your verbal defensive skills, and learn how to recognize criminal intent.

If the current climate leaves you feeling abandoned and defenseless, the *Shooter's Bible Guide to Home Defense* can put you on the path to becoming a proud sentry at the gates of your castle. Firearm expert Roger Eckstine examines how to evaluate the premises, how to choose various security systems, and how to safely interact with aggressors should someone invade your home.

$19.95 Paperback • ISBN 978-1-62636-179-9

Shooter's Bible Guide to Combat Handguns
by Robert A. Sadowski

For nearly one hundred years, *Shooter's Bible* has been the ultimate comprehensive resource for shooting enthusiasts across the board. Trusted by everyone from competitive shooters to hunters to those who keep firearms for protection, this leading series is always expanding. Here is the first edition of the *Shooter's Bible Guide to Combat Handguns*—your all-encompassing resource with up-to-date information on combat and defensive handguns, training and defensive ammunition, handgun ballistics, tactical and concealment holsters, accessories, training facilities, and more. No *Shooter's Bible* guidebook is complete without a detailed products section showcasing handguns from all across the market.

Author Robert Sadowski proves to be a masterful instructor on all aspects of handguns, providing useful information for every reader, from those with combat handgun experience in military and law enforcement fields to private citizens, first-timers, and beyond.

$19.95 Paperback • ISBN 978-1-61608-415-8

Shooter's Bible Guide to Firearms Assembly, Disassembly, and Cleaning
by Robert A. Sadowski

Shooter's Bible, the most trusted source on firearms, is here to bring you a new guide with expert knowledge and advice on gun care. Double-page spreads filled with photos and illustrations provide manufacturer specifications on each featured model and guide you through disassembly and assembly for rifles, shotguns, handguns, and muzzleloaders. Step-by-step instructions for cleaning help you to care for your firearms safely. Never have a doubt about proper gun maintenance when you own the *Shooter's Bible Guide to Firearms Assembly, Disassembly, and Cleaning*, a great companion to the original *Shooter's Bible*.

Along with assembly, disassembly, and cleaning instructions, each featured firearm is accompanied by a brief description and list of important specs, including manufacturer, model, similar models, action, calibers/gauge, capacity, overall length, and weight. With these helpful gun maintenance tips, up-to-date specifications, detailed exploded view line drawings, and multiple photographs for each firearm, the *Shooter's Bible Guide to Firearms Assembly, Disassembly, and Cleaning* is a great resource for all firearm owners.

$19.95 Paperback • ISBN 978-1-61608-875-0

Shooter's Bible Guide to Cartridges

Compiled and Edited by W. Todd Woodard

A guidebook designed specifically to teach gun users everything they need to know to select the right cartridge for their shooting needs, this title is written in an accessible and engaging style that makes research fun. The *Shooter's Bible Guide to Cartridges* is packed with full-color photographs, clear and detailed diagrams, and easy-to-read charts with cartridge data.

The *Shooter's Bible* name has been known and trusted as an authority on guns and ammunition for nearly one hundred years and has sold over seven million copies since its start. Now the *Shooter's Bible* offers readers this comprehensive and fascinating guide to cartridges. Complete with color and black-and-white photographs showcasing various makes and models of firearms and equipment, this guide to cartridges is the perfect addition to the bookshelf of any beginner or experienced hunter, firearm collector, or gun enthusiast. No matter what your shooting background is, you'll learn something new. This guide is a great introduction that will make readers want to seek out and get to know all the titles in the informative *Shooter's Bible* series.

$19.95 Paperback • ISBN 978-1-61608-222-2

Shooter's Bible Guide to Rifle Ballistics

by Wayne van Zwoll

Until you know what affects a bullet, you can't control its path. With *Shooter's Bible Guide to Rifle Ballistics*, you'll learn not only why bullets behave the way they do, but how you can make them hit exactly where you want. Here you'll also find a fascinating history of firearms—from the discovery of gunpowder to rifling, metallic cartridges, and optical sights. Look here for little-known details on rifle and ammunition manufacture. You'll get insights on rifle accuracy from the people who design and build rifles and ballisticians who've come up with the latest high-performance cartridges. Extensive ballistics tables let you compare your favorite cartridges and loads and show the effects of bullet shape in downrange energy and arc. Van Zwoll is as committed to sharing this information as he has been in collecting it over a lifetime of hunting and competitive shooting. His compelling, informal writing style makes this book read more like a story than a guide.

Heavily illustrated, this book not only tells you what works—it shows you. Photographs of the most effective equipment and shooting techniques and their results afield make this more than a treatise on ballistics: it's a page-turner for shooters at all points on the path to better marksmanship.

$19.95 Paperback • ISBN 978-1-61608-224-6

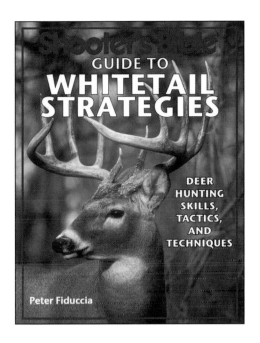

Shooter's Bible Guide to Whitetail Strategies
Deer Hunting Skills, Tactics, and Techniques
by Peter Fiduccia

Shooter's Bible Guide to Whitetail Strategies is the ultimate guide to hunting whitetail deer, from tracking strategies that include recovering wounded deer, to cooking with venison, to scoring and field-judging bucks. This book is the guide that every whitetail strategist must own. With Fiduccia's expert advice, both the novice and the seasoned hunter will have newfound confidence when heading out into the woods for a trophy buck.

$19.95 Paperback • ISBN 978-1-61608-358-8

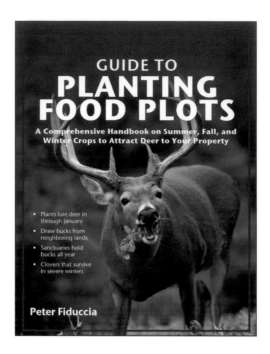

Shooter's Bible Guide to Planting Food Plots

A Comprehensive Handbook on Summer, Fall, and Winter Crops to Attract Deer to Your Property

by Peter Fiduccia

Planting a well-balanced, well-planned food plot for deer can be a great resource for any hunter: it attracts and holds deer in the area, and creates a healthier herd. This detailed, hands-on guide will teach you everything you need to know about planting food plots for deer like a pro. Author Peter Fiduccia shares the time-tested planting knowledge he has used on his farm to help anyone grow more successful food plots.

$19.95 Paperback • ISBN 978-1-62087-090-7